AF407407

DEVRET CLARKE
BEHIND THESE DOORS
YOU REALLY DON'T KNOW ANYBODY

BEHIND THESE DOORS
YOU REALLY DON'T KNOW ANYBODY

WRITTEN
BY:

DEVRET CLARKE

Copyright © 2022 Devret Clarke

All rights reserved

ISBN: 9798846590175
Imprint: Independently published

~ Peace and Blessings ~

*"**BEHIND THESE DOORS** - YOU REALLY DON'T KNOW ANYBODY", is all about the truth of who you think you know, I don't really think you know anything about them. People wear mask on a regular basis, some more than others. Personally, I don't wear mask, for I remain the same always, whether in front of my family, or in front of a total stranger. Honesty and truth is there. I want to help those who may think that they are clean, or those who have no clue of such things that they do, my voice can help you.*

As we witness on the news the horrific things that people have done unto their own flesh and blood, such as locking them in cages, and holding them there for their own disturbing desires, and pleasure. As you see what they do to their own, imagine all that they have done unto others? Read along to open up your mind to new areas of truth that can support your everyday life, in how you see others, and how you maintain your own life.

— Devret Clarke -
website:www.devretclarke.ca

CHAPTERS

CHAPTER
ONE
BEHIND THOSE DOORS

Mansions with nine too ten plus bedrooms. Condos with private laundry, and convenient living. Townhouses with four bedrooms, all with spacious living. Single standing houses with picket fences, and nice gardening surrounding the patio. When you look at a house, do you automatically think of a "happy home" because you see how nicely it is designed on the outside, and figure that the occupants of that household may appear happy? It is because you see the value of the house, and how green the grass is, that you believe it to be something great? Do the occupants automatically gain your trust, as well as care? Well, the only way to truly find out, is when you get behind those doors, for that is when you will know who the people truly are, and should only then shall you make your judgment upon entering, and exiting that household. Behind those doors comes many characters, and many personalities that you would never expect to ever witness in the flesh. This goes for the majority of people that are in the world.

Let me take you on a quick tour of my house, and let you get a glimpse of what it looks like being my doors. Well, the first thing you will notice once you enter my house, is pictures. Usually beginning with scripture verses. The first verse you will come across is Exodus 3:5 (KJV).

<u>S C R I P T U R E</u>
EXODUS 3:5
KING JAMES VERSION

5 And he said, Draw not nigh hither: put off thy shoes from off thy feet, for the place whereon thou standest is holy ground.

Having scripture verses upon my wall, is not only signs for people that enter my house to take off their shoes, but to also keep my place holy. I like to keep a clean house, having everything organized, and having a non-clustered environment. Being so, it prevents lots of filth build-up, incest, and even worse pest like mice, and rats. As you witness the cleanliness, you then will see pictures of family, being my loved ones, all throughout the walls of the house. I keep pictures up, not for show, but to remind me of how important family is. I also like the fact that memories can be displayed, and you can always remember the moment of where, and when the pictures were taken. Aside from that, you will expect the usual things that people have within their house(s), like furniture, bedding, and other necessities. I do have my own personal gym which has been in my life for my entire adulthood. It has gotten improved each time I invest into it, and now having so much that I am running out of space. Yet, the convenience is important to me. As much materialistic things that I have within my house, it all displays who I am as a man. As everything that I am about, is displayed within my house, I must say that I live a private lifestyle, and all that I show, displays my hobbies, interest, and personality, but only to those who I am in contact with often. I do not have much guest over. I do not host to just anyone really. Most guest that I have, are not guest but family members who can stop by at any time of the day or night. This is how I live. This is what you can expect behind my doors within my house. Notice I did not expose too much, nor shown pictures? For all that I do behind my walls, and my doors, is my business.

People tend to expose themselves more than they should. Many people are as myself, who are preserved, and not flashy at all, while keeping morals, and traditions the same, as their parents taught them. Growing up, we could rarely step into the house(s) of others. We knew our boundaries, and would only meet our friends at the front of their door. When we got the opportunity to enter someones house, we respected it as if we were in our own. There was rules to those opportunities. When you enter someone's house, the first thing you should do, is wish peace, and allow those to know that you come in the same way as you plan to leave. In peace.

SCRIPTURE
LUKE 10:5-6
KING JAMES VERSION

5 And into whatsoever house ye enter, first say, Peace be to this house.

6 And if the son of peace be there, your peace shall rest upon it: if not, it shall turn to you again.

The scripture used above is the best way to

enter someones house in peace. Being able to accept what they call "home", is important, and to bless it, is better to curse it. Peace is important to always have surrounding you, for many spirits are lurking, hoping to bring strife. I want peace where I live, and that includes surrounding my house as well. Sadly, there is people out there that actually enjoy drama, and wickedness surrounding them.

As you are in the home of a guest, you never tell anyone else about your stay, once leaving. You never gossip about how filthy, how clean, nor anything that doesn't need your criticism nor opinion, for you represent yourself, and how others will see you. You can build or break a connect that quick. We were taught to take off our shoes, and again, treat that house that you enter as your own. While in the house, never look down upon a man, but mind your own business, and know that the individual that allowed you in, doesn't deserve to be questioned about anything, knowing you are a guest. A simple understanding that all should understand is that we all live different, and all have their own rules, and regulations. All have their own custom way of living, and regard if you like the person, or not, you must respect those values, once entering that house. For example, as I've mentioned "shoes" often, you must take off your shoes whether the house iS filthy, or clean, for that is the rules to that house, unless appointed otherwise. If the parents of your friend is not home, then you can be bolder to ask about that house, but not to embarrass purposely. If you dislike how the place is kept, do not eat from anyone, nor drink from their glasses to prevent wasting their food, and making a face of disgust while eating, and drinking, which may just be taken offensive. Do not take anything that doesn't belong to you, nor be envious of what others have.

Many get "envy", and "admiring" mixed up all the time. Envy, is to be jealous, while admiring, is actually being impressed, and liking what you see, but not to desire.

S C R I P T U R E
EXODUS 20:17
KING JAMES VERSION

17 Thou shalt not covet thy neighbour's house, thou shalt not covet thy neighbour's wife, nor

13

his manservant, nor his maidservant, nor his ox, nor his ass, nor any thing that is thy neighbour's.

What is behind your doors? How you living? Continue to read on and experience how much changes you may make within your life, and how you see other people, while looking behind the doors of others. This doesn't only mean materialistic things, but how people are knowing your true home is your body, and mind. Lets see how good or evil, people are within themselves.

CHAPTER
TWO
THOSE HANDS
(THE FILTH THEREIN)

Would you eat from anybody? Would you sit down at a dinner table and share a meal from the person that lives next door to you? How many times have you eaten take out food? Are those clean hands really clean, when you clean your household? When you really take a moment to witness how filthy people's hand are, and by the time you get to the end of this chapter, I guarantee that you will not eat take out anymore, nor eat from other peoples house(s) that are not family, nor friends, ever again.

Being a picky individual, I try not to eat from just anyone. In fact, I only eat from my mother, and once and a while from fast food joints that are open 24/7 **only**, or are newly built within a few years old. Reason so, fast food companies that close before midnight, tend to have mice running around, and that can contaminate the food. While they tend to hire the youth, they will not mind serving you whatever is on the order, even if they see contamination upon the items. So, by ordering from a company that is open 24/7, you can have more security that there will not be pest at all, knowing there is active movement throughout the day, and night. Having frequent customers, means fresh food, compared to other companies that keep food stored for the next day, as they reuse the same ingredients to save time, and money. As I learned to cook from my mom, and even female friends of mine, I now handle my own food with the most care. Anyone eating from me, can ensure that their food is properly handled, for that is how my mother taught me, and allowed me to enjoy eating her food without concern. Washing hands often, and not leaving food exposed for too long is important. I also do not taste the food with the same spoon/fork that I am creating. Instead, I use multiple utensils when taste testing. Speaking of utensils, and plates, glass wear, I use brand new, and purchase brand new often. I will never use used items as so, knowing you really do not know how people live. I remember visiting an ex-girlfriends house, and she had so many different cups, I wondered how come? She told me that she typically goes to second hand companies, and as soon as I heard that, I never drank a single thing from her house, nor ate from her. As that relationship did not last long, due to other reasons, I have been taken aback when it comes to eating from other peoples house(s).

When I witnessed how people use their utensils, it was a huge turn off. I would witness people feeding their animal pets with the same spoons/forks, as what they use for themselves. How nasty is that? Even having their pets licking from the plate, after they are done eating a piece of cake, or seasoning sauce meal. Some people out there use the knives in the kitchen to scrape filth off of their shoes, and even kill incest, so having an understanding of who you are eating from is important. Knowing many people do not wash by hand, when cleaning, they use a dishwasher, and that doesn't take out the stains as you can with your hands/cloth/rag, that too is a turn off if witness the uncleanliness.

Now, going back to allowing animals to eat from your same plate, spoons/forks, is nasty due to the fact, animals lick themselves, and while outdoors on a walk, they sniff with their nose, while searching for food. While on that walk, I've been noticing dogs, and even cats, sniff fecal matter, and even having their nose so close that it appears to be touching it. How many pet owners wipe their dogs/cats nose while entering their house again? Not many. How about their feet/paws? Lets slow it down, and look at what I just wrote. When you enter my house, I expect for you to take off your shoes, as stated before, knowing outside has much filth, and your shoes can pick up many unclean things, from spit, too vomit/barf, too dog crap. It can soil your household flooring/carpet. So, as people with pets, how do they get a pass? How do animals get a pass over humans? They deserve no pass whatsoever. I've witnessed a lot of people allowing their pets to sleep in the same bed with themselves, which is just as filthy. Aside from that, even the owners of those pets walking inside with shoes on, and putting their feet up on their bed, couch, and coffee table. Side not, have you ever thrown away your socks after entering someone's house? It's that bad that you take off your shoes, and feel the filth under your socks, and upon leaving, you have to put your socks back into your shoes. Form that point on, you are grossed out, while seeing all the crap on your sock bottom. I had to throw my socks out a few times after entering places I would go to look on for rental purposes. The ones with the best were the worst.

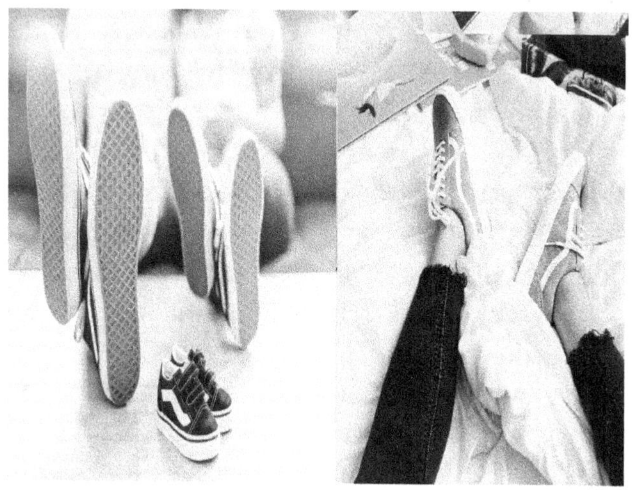

What do most humans do while going to their bed? Not bathe? Sure, so what gives an animal a pass? I can assure you that no one out there, bathes their pets daily. Instead they allow that filthy animal to sleep with them on their sheets. Even sitting on their couch. Think about a dog going to the bathroom, compared to a human. That animal is an animal for a reason, and doesn't use toilet paper, nor washes itself, because it doesn't need to, being an animal. As a human, what is your excuse to not cleaning your animal(s), and even yourself the same? You would more get upset if your spouse has not showered before bed, but would not mind a filthy dog, that goes to the washroom, licks itself, and tends to lick you in the face. That is disgusting.

It's worse when you witness someone with a pet that soils their sheets, and couches, and even car seats while having guest over. I remember being offered a ride by a co-worker who had nothing but pet hair and stains upon the seat of the car. It was so bad, I had to decline the ride, and walk. Worse, it was a rainy day, which made the co-worker feel bad, however, I felt more clean walking in the rain than sitting on that seat. Apart of my process while seeking a mate when younger, a huge thing for me was that I would not want to date anyone with a dog, for the selected reasons listed above. Just to avoid conflict. My parents had pets, but they were always left outside, throughout any weather within Jamaican, where they are from. I believe building a shed is the best proper way to store your animals, and if inside, treat them as a human baby, by bathing, and keeping it clean often. Not to come off racist, but knowing Caucasians have dogs the most, they tend to smell like their pets, even while not with them, for they sleep with them, and do not bathe them often as much as they should. It's not a good smell, especially when they are in the rain. Being honest, take this as a hint over disrespect, for I'm only being honest/real. The saying you are what you eat, may be true, but what is more true, is you are what you sleep with, and live with.

Touching back on the subject of food, and hands. I wanted to also bring in the fact that pet owners, especially dog owners tend to pick up after their dogs, while using the see-through small bags. You can witness them waving it around like a trophy. When fluids come from our body, it comes off with heat. Whether you are doing a number one (1), or a number two (2). Heat is what comes out with it. Those who pick up after their dogs, though appreciated, still, have that stench of shit on their hands, and everything they touch is spread germs.

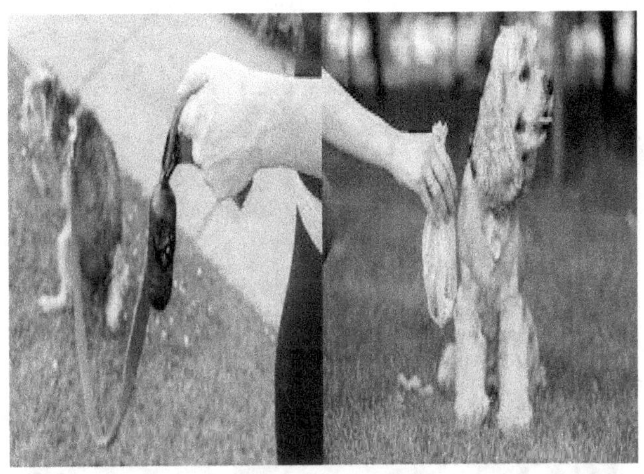

They dig right in to that pile of crap while that dog leaves its load on the grass, even while kicking it in the process with its hind legs. If I had a pet, I'm making sure to use a long stick, and one that is attachable and reusable. Most dog owners walk with their dog and load for blocks until they see the nearest garbage can. I've even witnessed people walking past garbage bins, while holding that baggy with them, and it annoys me, knowing I question where do they plan on bringing that? Even when they walk past me, as I tend to take long walks often. It's always a game of choose the opposite side down the path, just to not accidentally be hit while walking by, and hitting hand with the dog owner.

Touching back on the subject of hands and food, how many make sure to wash their hands straight-way, while entering back into their house? How many actually live in a building, and touch the doors that everyone must go through? This is not a good thing. Imagine being with someone with a dog, and coming home with forgetting to wash up, and reaching for your face, or straightway into the kitchen, while preparing your next meal. How secure are you about your partners cleanliness/hygiene? Picture some grapes finger fed onto you, or your spouse digging their hand into a bag of chips that you are eating at that present moment. Yuk! I remember living in a building with a nasty building representative workers that could not understand cleanliness. There was a female worker who would use the same dirty rag to wipe down everything she passed, while doing her routine. It was so disgusting to witness. She started in the laundry room, where she would wipe down the top of the washers, and dryer machines. Then she would wipe down sink with the same cloth, and I mean inside the sink where people spit, and do all sorts of stuff. She then would make her way to inside the machines, yet again with the same cloth, and wearing no gloves at all. If she were to see something on the floor, she would use that same cloth to wipe it up, and even pick the mysterious items up without considering what it was. From that point on, she would sweep, and use her hands to pull off all the hair that was on the bottom of the broom. How do you even after that? From that point on, she would again reach out for that filthy rag, while wiping down the door handles. I would watch her, because I had to plan my escape out of that laundry room without touching anything she touched, just to avoid any form of germs on my supposedly clean clothes. It's like going to the public washroom, everyone knows to use your shoes or a piece of paper to flush the toilet, and touch the handles. I felt sorry for those who used the laundry machines after she cleaned it, knowing all the filth, including dead bugs (roaches), would be in the machines dissembled body parts, as witnessed. From being so grossed out, I made sure to wash my clothes at my mom's house, even if it was a half an hour away.

Lets take it a bit further, and witness how people that work for companies, not only have pets, but also do not keep themselves clean. Many pick at their face often. Whether it be their nose, their zits, their teeth, ears, and/or the crust in between their eyes. Many tend to look at whatever comes from such areas, as witnessed many times while I used to take public transit. What are they looking for? It has become such a gross thing that whenever I would encounter such people doing such things in public, I would count the amount of seconds it took for them to stop looking at the treasure they found, before they disposed of it. It has gotten that bad, but luckily for me, I no longer take public transit. Those hands are filthy, and many even touch the rail while standing, or getting up, to enter/leave the bus/train, ext. Same thing applies to drivers. I've seen so many people going deep into their nose while cruising down the streets.

The Most High told us through IIIS prophets that we should pick the mote out of our own eyes, before we judge another, so let me state some good ways to keep clean, and prevent being so filthy. (See MATTHEW 7:1-5).

When I wake up in the morning, I am just like everyone else, and have build up of gunk on my face, nose, ears, where ever. I know that I do not want my hands to touch anywhere. So, I use q-tips which are cotton on both ends of a stick, while having a inner handle. I use such things to clean my nose, ears, and even the cold within the inner portions of the eyes. Using cotton often to wipe away grease and such things, to prevent myself from later having to use my hands, especially in public, because for one, it's not going to make me feel good knowing I touched public areas, and then touching my face. For two, no one needs to witness such things from other individuals. Again, the public transit is a prime example. I've witnessed people flossing their teeth on the bus before, and even using nail clippers with nails flying all over the place. I've witnessed people picking their nose, and ears often, while rolling it in their fingers. Ugh! I've witness people put such disgust in places that they should not have done so, nor having anything to wipe off their hands, they would tend to use the seat next to them. Most of these people are working class people, and may just be your server at your local restaurant, so think on that for a moment. How pleasant would you take it, if you were to go to your favourite eating spot, to see the chef is that same individual on the bus who you saw doing such unpleasant things?

It is important that we take care of our health, and care for the heath of others. When I think about hands, I think how dirty they are. So much people use their hands to touch surfaces that are used frequently. From door handles, shopping carts, and even ATM machines. We tend to touch what others touch often, The biggest germs you can find is within coins, and bills, the money that is our currency. From hand to hand, and places that you will not even imagine, that money is everywhere. I remember having to use a hanger to take money out of the toilet bowl one time. It was a big amount, and that is why I couldn't allow it to go down the drain. Though there was nothing in the toilet alongside it, still, no one would want to hold that money if they knew where it came from. I had to put it in an envelope and just throw it on the counter, while making a purchase. Funny thing is, I most likely touched that money again in circulation, for it would not be that hard for it to happen. Yet, what you don't see won't hurt you.

Speaking on money, I look at people going to eat in a food court, within a crowded shopping centre/mall. As a kid, I would go and purchase my food, and sit down, while enjoying the meal, while forgetting to wash my hands before eating. It comes off as hard to do, while you are in a public place, and would not want to leave your food unattended. How often do you get wet wipes alongside your meal? Again, not too often, and quite rarely. If ever I purchase fast food, rarely, I do not sit and eat in general public places, such as a cafeteria/food courts. I bring my food back home. I would never eat on a bus either, knowing there is too many particles going around from other passengers, and dust can certainly enter your food. Even smells, for you do not want to smell foul odour while in a bus full of people, while you chow down on your food. For it will feel as if it is entering your mouth.

What about the cashiers when ordering your food? I had to yell at a few while ordering my food. I came off as an ass-hole, however, you must understand the position that they put me in. Do I stand back, and say nothing, while I notices that cashier tending to the register, and then going back without washing hands, and the use of gloves to touch items, which are needed to be prepared? It didn't hurt me as much, to say something, rather than getting sick from the filthy money that she touched.

She could have taken it personal, but it was the money that was my problem. I may as well walk around the entire food court, and let every stranger touch that food, and then consume it, if I were to allow her to prepare my food without washing up first.

There are people out here that do worse with their hands, and what they do may just make you · think twice before eating from just anyone. I look at hands as public seats on a bus. How clean are those seats? Better yet, how clean are the asses that sit on those seats that you end up sitting on? From soiled underwear, too females having that time of the month, periods juice. Ewe! Maybe it is just me, but I would rather stand at times, especially if someone just got off of that seat freshly. Let it air out and take the heat away, for when you go and sit right away, it's hot, and that person butt sweat much have been all over it. Nothing worse than sitting on a hot seat with someone with sweaty ass cheeks. Ha ha, jokes aside, think about hands. Think about where they go? Think about the things that I refuse to touch on, however, let me just state the fact that some people touch insects, rodents, dead or alive, and do not practice clean washing of the hands. I remember witnessing someone pick up a rat by the tail, without gloves, and that individual worked for a fast food company. I remember witnessing a female in public reach deep into her backside, pulling it out, and taking sniff for what ever reason. Again, ewe! Picture her making your sub of the day? How gross is that?

Do you know your chefs? Do you trust all men/women? With those questions asked, is the same reason I found the answer to stop buying from just anyone. I do not go out often, and when I do, I would rather starve, and wait until I get back home to eat, than to sample from just anywhere. People are not as clean as you may think and when you start thinking about such things, you will value the time, and effort that it takes to prepare your own meals. I think about rice, and as basic as it is, it is extremely dirty. I also think about lettuce insects within the layers of the leaves. If both of the listed foods are not cleaned properly, they will not be such a desire. I know this, because I prepare both often. Rice, has a lot of dirt within it. It has a lot of particles that you need to sift through in order to clean. Imagine being at a restaurant eating rice, while it is seasoned with soy sauce or something, how would you know if it was washed? Most companies would just throw it in the pot without washing, and sifting through it. As I cut lettuce at home, I noticed that my knife would slice between a caterpillar/worm, and it would be uneatable. Again, imagine a fast food restaurant that doesn't wash your lettuce, how do you know they didn't include those worms that tend to grow within it? I can't forget about eggs. Some have blood in them, and many take the eye out, which most restaurants would not care. Luckily for me, I no longer eat eggs, knowing it's basically a fetus.

Not everyone cares. Most people want to make it through the day, especially when it comes to working, so you can never expect every place to upkeep/uphold such standards, and there is no way of you finding out the truth, even upon asking, for they will always give the right answer to soothe your pleasantness. We all know that workers that work in restaurants tend to work long shifts, and use the washroom often. I highly doubt how people carry themselves clean while taking care of their business at work. In my younger years, I would read peoples post online about "rants & raves", where workers that worked in restaurants would state how they never washed their hands on purpose, while using the rest room at work. They stated how they done so on purpose, or due to being rushed on the job. As a man that needs trust to be earned, I can't trust these companies out here that make food too often, knowing people are the reason for such cases happening, and trust will never be earned. Most cases, I order chicken, and fries, knowing the workers do not touch it at all with their hands. Anything else, is off limits for me, especially pizza. Think about a worker with hairy fingers, and sweating hands kneading the dough to your pizza? Think about those same hand picking at a scab on their face, or body?. Anything that comes from their hands, including the finger nails, will be in your pizza. No thank you!

The next time you go out to the restaurant, make sure to stay far away from ordering such items to prevent the uncleanliness of these companies/individuals. Or, order what you like, eat it peacefully. Enjoy. For those who work in such places, please make sure to wash your hands frequently, and do not serve what you would not want another serving unto you. Food is consumed, and should be handled with care. Whether you like your company that you work for or not, treat people as you would like to be treated. For the protection of those who support your business/company, and even pay you, we all deserve clean food.

WASH YOUR HANDS!

CHAPTER
THREE
BEHIND THOSE DOORS PART 2
(KNOW WHERE TO LIVE,
KNOW THY NEIGHBOURS)

The first thing that I want to state is that, those who live next door to you, are not considered your neighbour(s). This mainly goes for Israelites (Blacks, African Americans, Negroes), those who were taken away from their own land, and scattered throughout the world. This doesn't apply to all, but the majority, for we live in a place that our forefathers never settled upon on their own. Stolen from our home land, and also forced to live amongst the heathen, we are not here by will, but by force. And so, those that live next door to us, is not by choice but due to the circumstances. If you live in Jamaica, and surrounding islands, you can certainly considered those people living among you as brothers, and sisters, your true neighbours, knowing there is no other nation of people that live there as the majority.

Now, as that is put aside and out of the way, try your best to stay away from the worst set of people that are set against us, and they are the Edomites (Caucasians). Never live among them, nor feel secure around them, for they are nothing but trouble. Their intentions are to obtain control, power, and always try to feel like they own you, as well as your property. Whether you rent, or own, they will try to control everything. If you have a choice to live somewhere, try to live in places that are within your own culture, and nationality. For one, you can understand the ways of the people, and for another reason being, you will get along most with them, which matters most, and you are safe around your own.

As you can see with the communities within North America that are established, being financially, and witness how each community is surviving, while uniting, and looking out for themselves, as they keep the peace. This may not apply much to our people, knowing our people were lost for so long, due to being robbed of our true selves, and everything that is our own, from our GOD, our beliefs, our foundation that our ancestors have lived, due to slavery. We are now being forced to adapt and comply with the ways of the heathen. Our laws, statutes, and commandments that the Most High has given to our forefathers, and passed on to each of the generations, we are instead upholding the ways of these heathen, while following their laws, and they are against us on many angles.

Now, due to experience, I believe the best place to live is within a home. As long as you live with family, or close friends of the same race. It is important to have, and you will most likely feel most at peace there. Working together to build and unify all that is necessary to be structured, have stability, as well as the capabilities to maintain. When I say a "home", I mean within a townhouse, or single family house, or even a semi-detached house. These will leave you with more privacy, more space, and better living. You do not want to settle living in any form of building. From condos, to regular buildings, these are going to be trouble, one way or another. If you are living among a lot of different cultures/races of people, you must understand everyone lives different due to their own customs. Be ready to smell their cooking, listen to their music, and even hear them speak in their native tongue. The worst people to live next to are Caucasians, and this is not hate, but due to the fact that they are our known enemies that peruse us often. They care for what we do, only to place judgment, and try to control, compared to other nations. They would rather try to spend as much time harassing you, and hoping for you to be annoyed by them. They hate our lifestyles so much that they think they have a pass to correct our life choices. For example, they attack our characters, and personalities often. They hate our attire, and the way that we dress. They dislike our crafts, and choice of music. They only enjoy such things when they have their pockets full, while using and oppressing our people, for self gain. The hate that they have for us is Biblical. And it is perpetual hatred, which is one sided mostly, for they are the pursuers, and cannot seem to leave us alone. They hate us without a cause, and only wish the worst for us. It's as if they do not want us to excel over them. This is a fact, knowing I live in Toronto, and have witnessed the Chinese, the Asians rise up above, even the Indians, over Caucasians financially, and with more equity, yet these Edomites have no beef per se with them. They do not care as much compared to if our people would rise higher than them. These Edomites (Caucasians) have been keeping a close grip upon our people, and have been trying to keep us oppressed, and without. Just as long as they are ahead of us, they will not care so much for the other nations. They have their foot upon our neck, and we should understand that by living next to them, we will only be in constant battles, and defending ourselves often, as well as dealing with false claims, defamation, and invasion of privacy, as well as them monitoring our every movement when it concerns shovelling of snow, and mowing the lawn. All things must be up to date, and on their time frame. I can't recall a time in my life, where Blacks (Israelites) were first to cause trouble, and throw the first stone towards Caucasians, nor any other race of people. We are not in their way at all, and never have been. During the "freedom" of slavery, they only became mad, and angry, while having us released from their bondage, to an extent, and instead they would prefer to have a yoke of bondage around our neck, working for free, so that they don't have to, and in their property.

The things that I've witnessed them do, is terrible. We as Israelites (Blacks, African Americans, and Negroes) would never waste time doing the things that they do unto us. In fact, our people would rather harm our own, and hold back our own, instead of attempting to harm that Edomite Nation. Overall, when it comes to petty things, we do not waste time doing such things at all, compared to the childish behaviours of adults within the nation of Edom.

While living within a building, they will think of the entire building as one unit, and expect for you to greet them as if they are someone you knew, or as if they were important. If that were the case, why not behave the same way everywhere you go, and greet every single person you pass on the street? It's the simple-minded fools that don't understand this. There is nothing wrong with "hello", but you should never expect it, nor get in your feelings if someone doesn't say such things onto you. In fact, if you live right next door to them, they feel even closer, as if you should be friends. I like my privacy, and if I could choose who I want to live next door to, I sure would not want to live next door to certain people, and as someone in the truth that knows good from evil, I would never want to live next door to the seeds of Satan.

Again, if you choose to live in a building/condo, due to not being able to afford a house to rent/own, aim to live next door to people with children, as you can have more privacy than anything, knowing the distraction of the noise will blot out any eavesdroppers hoping to invade your phone calls, and conversations with your guest over. I've had the worst case, where every time I went on the phone, everything went silent surrounding my unit. Everyone on that floor, closest to my unit would purposely come out of their unit, just to come around and listen. Yes, the walls are that hallow, and thin. It was worse when you can't even use the bathroom without having your privacy stripped. I caught on occasion, a few grown adults with their ears to my wall, while living on the first floor. They were that nosy, and yes, they were Caucasians.

As kids are noise and rowdy, it is best to live beside them, rather than under them. For beside them, the noise will be loud frequently, however, if living underneath them, good luck on having your peace. Kids will be kids. Still, it plays as "white noise", while you live in your apartment/condo. It may not be so great once it's time for bed though.

There is something about being nosy, being a problem for many people today. Privacy has been stripped from so many lives, due to perverted people, you can never really have that peace again. The extreme levels that such evil people take, is nasty, and horrible. As many people want to live their lives, they do not want to have total strangers, trying to invade their privacy, when there is no purpose in them doing so. It's just as bad as going to war with someone who you never met before, but has a grudge over your own life, while they cling onto it, hoping to find some form of life through you. People will go the distance just to find dirt on you, and attempt to exploit you for the fame. The worst kind of people to live around are those who just want to fit in with the hype, and gossip. Especially when it is against you. I am not one to sit around listening to weak individuals talk trash about other people. I am not one to want to care for someone in the negative, rather than the positive. So when someone comes around trying to bring dirt on another for me to hear, I do what ever I can to shut down that conversation, and keep it moving. No one seems to ever want to spread positive rumours. It's always negative, for negativity appears to be more flattering to many, while the positive, doesn't last long, and only exposes those gossiping, as losers, who can't share the same good news.

You can talk about me, and find the worst thing about my life, while the amount of good that I do, will never be mentioned due to hate, and haters. When someone has bad intentions for you, don't expect for them to speak any kind of good on your name. By talking good about an enemy, will only make you come off ignorant, and without purpose to hate. Picture this, "a man just donated to charity, his reward, after coming to the rescue of children in a burning bus", "The man saved the life of a bus full of children, however could not make it in time to save the bus driver, who died in the fire. That man has gotten many donations for his good deeds". Your enemy will hear that and say nothing positive, knowing they are your enemies. Yet, they will try to find an excuse to make you out as the bad guy, taking away from who you truly are, by saying, "why would he give away the reward, even though he never deserved it due to not saving the bus driver.", "that bus driver's family should have gotten something out of those donations, not him".

Just to show you how evil people in this world can be. Not everything is worth commenting on, nor giving an opinion. Keeping your mouth closed is ideal for many situations, yet, so many speak loosely, while trying to bring negative energy where ever they go. With all said, it is best to live surrounding our own, family is best. In a house, and away from ignorant people. I recommend visiting the area where you plan to live, and even witness who are the people that live next door to you. Knowing you may not know who lives beside you in a building, you can certainly ask the building representatives, if they tell the truth. Speaking on building representatives, never live next door to them either. They will try to control all that you do within your own unit. If you plan on listening to music, they will be the first to complain, and try to tell you how you should listen to your music, how you should cook, and how you should live overall. They may just be looking to fill a vacant apartment to keep their job, and get money from it, so don't expect them to be kind, and pleasant to live next to, nor want to have as the representatives. It's best to live in a place where there is no building representatives, but upper management only. The worst case, which is expected, is having someone move into a unit that you don't like, or is a nasty person to live next too, due to their wicked, and uncleanliness ways.

Many childish adults can't behave themselves, nor move in respect, so they do such evil unto your belongings, and sabotage, and tamper all that belongs to you. Whether it is your laundry, your car, or if you have troubles with the building representatives, they will invade your privacy, while entering your unit while you are not present at home. They will snoop around, and eavesdrop upon you, and even steal from you. Some tenants within a building will stomp the floors above your heard, and make lots of noise on purpose, to annoy you, and ultimately do so to drive you out of your unit. Believe me, this has happened to me. There are some truly nasty individuals out here in this world, that are ignorant, childish, selfish, and one-sided, simple-minded, and hateful towards others, typically while hiding behind those doors. Nothing you can truly do about that, while living in a condo/building, and with that said, I would recommend having a house that is not attached. You have your property and what is yours, is yours. While living in a building, being too close to other people, they behave oddly, and ignorantly, to the point where they feel like they can get away with such evil, while hiding, and blaming other tenants for their own disgusting behaviours. Since so, many have now had their privacy stripped from them.

Lets now take a closer look inside of these heathens houses, as we go behind those doors to expose the ways of the wicked.

CHAPTER
FOUR
BEHIND THOSE DOORS PART 3
(A CLOSER LOOK INSIDE)

I wanted to now allow you to witness how evil man can be, and force ourselves through the doors of many. Those who have been caught doing the unbelievable, and unthinkable. Those who have been caught in situations of wickedness, while behind walls/doors that are not pleasant places to be behind if you are them, nor the people that have to deal with them. The only reason they deserve to get their privacy stripped, is due to the fact that they have done evil onto another.

I want to first bring to your attention that there are numerous stories with the same kind of situations, and it is typically from the same nation of people doing such things, and I will try my best to give the best description possible. These heathen deserve to keep their shame upon them, while I would post their pictures, however, knowing my name is on the front of this book, I will not display such worthlessness that will never leave this book of mine. Instead I will leave pictures of the situations of those being held captive, and had to face.

Lets look at this case that happened in 2020, in Alabama. Three suspects, all being Caucasians (Edomites), had four children locked up, and suffering. Below is the stories. I will put a few of the cases up, and then touch on each of them separately.

***"4 children were locked in makeshift cages, Alabama police say. 3 people have been arrested"* (Source: CNN).**

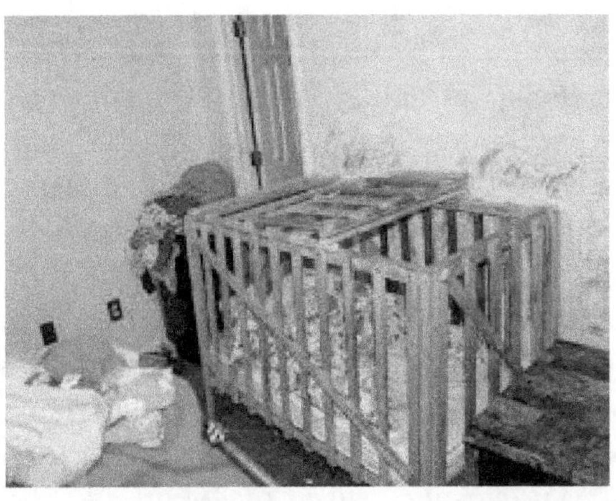

"Three people have been arrested and face child abuse charges for allegedly locking four children between the ages of 3 and 11 in makeshift cages, the Lee County Sheriff's

Office said Wednesday.

Investigators got a tip Monday about possible child abuse at a home in Smiths Station, the sheriff's office said in a news release. They made a welfare check and found four children, ages 3, 4, 10 and 11. Authorities also saw two wooden cages outfitted with locks and fasteners, the sheriff's office said.

"Investigation revealed evidence that the children had been locked in the cages on multiple occasions," . The news release said. Pamela Deloris Bond, 66; James H. Bond, 69; and Kylla Michelle Mann, 30, each faces two counts of aggravated child abuse of a child younger than 6 and two counts of reckless endangerment, the sheriff's office said. Pamela Bond also is charged with tampering with physical evidence. The three are being held on more than $120,000 bond each. A fifth child, an 8-month-old, also lived at the home, authorities said, but wasn't there during the welfare check. All of the children are in the care of the Lee County Department of Human Resources, which had personnel on hand

during the welfare check. .

As you can see in the case above, three Caucasians, so called parents, and daughter who were so evil to harm their own children while tormenting them. How can anyone considered locking up their child in a cage? It makes you wonder because people tend to cherish their pets, mainly dogs, more than their babies. It's such a shame that people would do so such things unto another person, which is must worse, on to their own. Lets continue unto the next case.

Craigslist killer once kept sex slave chained in basement: (Source *John Agar)*| *WYOMING, MI - Shortly before he tortured and killed a young, pregnant woman, Craigslist killer Brady Oestrike kept another woman chained in his basement as a sex slave, police reports say. The woman escaped his house on Taft Avenue SW. She said Oestrike kept chains around her neck and was obsessed with using a Taser on her. She initially thought this was part of "slave/bondage role playing" but began to fear for her safety. Wyoming*

Police on Wednesday, Nov. 2, released police reports in the July 2014 killings of Brooke Slocum, 18, and Charles Oppenneer, 25, in response to Freedom of Information Act requests.

Oestrike, 31, shot and killed himself as police closed in during a July 17, 2014, vehicle chase. Oestrike beheaded Oppenneer. He abducted and tortured Slocum, who was eight months pregnant, over the course of five days before he killed her, too, police reports say. He met the couple at Gezon Park after corresponding on Craigslist. He was to pay them for sex. Weeks earlier, Oestrike had developed another relationship with a woman he met on Craigslist, police reports show. The woman had placed a personal ad seeking for friendship and sex. She also described sexual activity that was blacked out on police reports. Oestrike responded to her ad within an hour. She received 27 other inquiries. She and Oestrike shared emails and telephone numbers. She told Oestrike she lived in Coldwater but wanted to move. Oestrike said she could move in with him. In mid-May 2014, he drove to Coldwater. He asked if the woman would ride back in a suitcase. She found the request strange but thought it was part of a "kinky sexual act and she agreed to," police wrote. After two hours, the car stopped. She believed that Oestrike drugged her. He opened a zipper and sprayed something into the suitcase. She was groggy. He carried her in the suitcase into his house. He asked her to be his sex slave, she told police. She saw several security cameras, including one in the bathroom. The cameras were for security, he said. He told her he was paranoid. He showed her a gun. He put it to her head. He then put a metal chain, attached to the basement floor, around her neck. She agreed to his demand that they have sex. He ignored her requests to stop. She said living conditions inside the home were deplorable. The kitchen was messy, with expired food in the refrigerator. Sticky floors were covered with piles of clothes. She spent two days making it livable. When Oestrike left for work, he would chain her by the neck. Once, when she said she was sick, and asked him not to chain her up, he shocked her with a stun gun. He held the Taser on her for 20 seconds. It was his "ultimate fantasy," police reports said. She said she feared for her life. On June 19, 2014, the woman was free to call 911. It is unclear what happened after that but she went to a facility for a week, refusing contact with Oestrike before she moved into a domestic-violence shelter".

As you can see in the case above, this guy being Caucasian as well, living a messed up life. Shame on that female who decided to be apart of his sick and twisted games, but that game turned fatal for a few of them. As she escaped, it wasn't so good for others. This just goes to show you how people out here are living behind those doors, and it is nothing good. Torment, and torture is pleasure to these heathen. Lets look at the next one which sound similar, Maybe they are related.

Man Admits Keeping 5 Women in Bunker as Sex Slaves (<u>New York Times Article</u>) - *June 11, 2003 A retired handyman known as a local eccentric pleaded guilty today to charges that he kidnapped five women and held them captive in a bunker under his suburban yard* *so he could force them to have sex. The retiree, John Jamelske, 68, admitted in Onondaga County Court here that he kidnapped the women, ranging in age from 14 to one in her early 50's, over the last 15 years. The first victim, a 14-year-old girl, was taken in 1988 and held for three years, the authorities said; the last, age 16, was kidnapped in October 2002 and rescued on April 7 this year. They were kept captive one at a time, and all but the last were released by Mr. Jamelske. Prosecutors said that Mr. Jamelske told them last month he decided to kidnap the women after his ailing wife, Dorothy, was no longer able to have sex. "His reason was that he wanted a sexual relationship with monogamous partners who he was sure were not out getting diseases," said the first chief assistant district attorney, Rick Trunfio. Dorothy Jamelske died in 1999, and the kidnappings continued, Mr. Trunfio said. The defense lawyer, J. Michael Forsyth, said Mr. Jamelske had been at first reluctant to accept blame for his actions, seeming to believe that the relationships were consensual because the women had not seized every opportunity to escape.*

Similar to the one previous. What's wrong these these guys? Again this was a Caucasian doing this. I'm not being hateful, but if you were to take a basic Internet search, you will come across these same stories that are accessible for all to access. I"ve also come across so many people, Caucasians mainly, luring little children into their cars with candy, and money. They seem to not be able to get women. Here is a case of incest, and maybe that is another reason why some of them can't get women, and even have to go as bad as to be with their own sisters/brothers.

A CASE OF INCEST (Source: Murderpedia) *- Born May 12, 1942, Eddie Lee Sexton was an abusive and incestuous father who forced his children into a murderous lifestyle. Sexton gave his children a childhood filled with trauma and shocking levels of abuse by creating a cult-like family system. His lifestyle was influenced by his unorthodox religious beliefs that were an amalgamation of occultist practices, Satanism, and Christian* *fundamentalism. Along with his wife, Estella Sexton, Eddie would regularly expose his children to physical and sexual abuse. Influenced by a life filled with incestuous sexual abuse, some of the children began to be sexually abusive towards their siblings as well. Eventually, Eddie impregnated his daughter Pixie and made her marry Joel, an unsuspecting high school classmate, to cover up the crime.*

Over time, the Sexton family began to raise suspicions and prompted law enforcement to gather details and create a file on the family. However, there was not enough evidence to prosecute until Eddie's daughter, Machelle, reported that her father had raped her. Machelle later retracted her statement, but her initial statement caused some of the Sexton family children to be placed in foster homes where unarguable evidence was procured that the Sexton children were being abused. Eventually, the family ran from law enforcement and began to change their location consistently to evade the police. Ultimately, the cycle of abuse and incest led to the murder of the father-son duo of Skipper and Joel, Eddies grandson and son-in-law. On January 14, 1994, authorities arrested Eddie and Estella Sexton from a location in Florida. They were given death sentences after some of the children testified to details of abuse and sexual violence. Official sources declared Eddie as the grand mastermind behind the entire cult-like operation filled with incest and murder.

You must be a complete piece of shit, and lonely to be so desperate to have to do such a crime against your own children. Again, this is another Caucasian that has committed such evil. This makes me wonder how Black people (Israelites) have so much bad stereotypes, while these heathen seem to always get a pass while doing the unthinkable? Maybe it is because they claim "crazy" when caught, or is it because no one is paying such things much attention?

The Horrifying Story Of Elisabeth Fritzl — Who Spent 24 Years In Her Father's Prison

<u>(Source:The Guardian)</u> *August 28, 1984, 18-year-old Elisabeth Fritzl went missing.*

Her mother Rosemarie hastily filed a missing-persons report, frantic over the whereabouts of her daughter. For weeks there was no word from Elisabeth, and her parents were left to assume the worst. Then out of nowhere, a letter arrived from Elisabeth, claiming she had grown tired of her family life and run away.

Her father Josef told the policeman who came to the house that he had no idea where she would go, but that she likely joined a religious cult, something she had talked previously about doing. But the truth was that Josef Fritzl knew exactly where his daughter was: she was about 20 feet below where the police officer was standing.

On August 28, 1984, Josef called his daughter into the basement of the family's home. He was re-fitting a door to the newly renovated cellar and needed help carrying it. As Elisabeth held the door, Josef fixed it into place. As soon as it was on the hinges, he swung it open, forcing Elisabeth inside and knocking her unconscious with an ether-soaked towel.

For the next 24 years, the inside of the dirt-walled cellar would be the only thing Elisabeth Fritzl would see. Her father would lie to her mother and the police, feeding them stories about how she'd run away and joined a cult. Eventually, the police investigation into her whereabouts would run cold and before long, the world would forget about the missing Fritzl girl.

Again, though not incest, another story about

another Caucasian man keeping his own child hostage, and treating that child like shit. It's such a shame what can be behind those doors. I tried to look for non-Caucasian but could not find such cases. The worst Black people do is kill over drugs or money, and at times kill innocent children, while dry-by's. Though still evil, and wicked, I count them out when it comes to doing such kidnapping, and torture. If money is not involved, Black will not be apart of it, nor have that mentality to be so cruel. Caucasians have proven time after time what they are capable of doing, even while doing the most disturbing things during slavery. We must expose such things, for there is worse cases going around the world with human trafficking, and captivity, that has not been captured nor exposed. Maybe the after effect of slavery was worse for those who held slaves, more than the slaves themselves, knowing there is a lot of recent cases proving so. The Israelites, are healing from the pain we were inflicted with, however, it was prophecy, so what is the excuse of these heathen who never had the curse set over them from the Most High, to be in such scenarios? This is all man's actions towards his own lust, and sin, towards self, and others. Lets continue with two more.

Louisiana woman found dead in shocking neglect case, 'melted' into couch (Source: New York Post / *NOLA.com*) - *A 36-year-old Louisiana woman who suffered from locked-in syndrome was found dead in her parents' home — with her emaciated and feces-covered body "melted" into the couch.*

The body of Lacey Ellen Fletcher was found Jan. 3 sunken into a hole in the living room couch at the Slaughter home of Lacey Fletcher and her parents, Sheila and Clay Fletcher, Sheila called 911 that morning from the home on Tom Drive, where responding police officers encountered a gruesome scene and a strong stench, District Attorney Sam D'Aquilla told the outlet. In what officials said was one of the worst cases of neglect in memory, the East Feliciana Parish coroner ruled Lacey's shocking death a homicide – leading to a criminal investigation. "The caretakers just let her sit on the couch. She just urinated and used the bathroom on the couch," D'Aquilla told NOLA.com this week.

Need I say more? How evil is that? How can one pass by that woman each and every day, while not wanting to aid her existence? Did they sit next to her on that couch, eating a sandwich? How can anyone tolerate that smell, and stench that is there? How can anyone work for that household, while witnessing such things, and not reporting it? It goes to show you how evil people truly are, and how wicked the lives of many be, as well as, how human decency no longer exist for so many out there. To see the photo, you will only be lost of words. Below is the couch she died in, or as they said, "melted in".

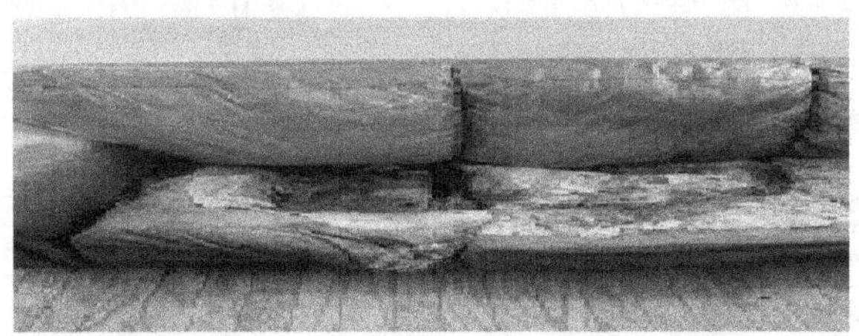

Florida mom accused of keeping child with autism in cage <u>(Source: NewYork Dailynews.com)</u> - *A Florida mom was arrested this week after cops searched her bug-infested*

home and learned she was keeping a child with autism locked in a makeshift cage, authorities said. Melissa Doss, 43, told officers she made the cage with wire and wood to prevent her daughter from escaping at night as the girl suffers from severe autism, according to police. Cops found the large cage Sunday while investigating possible child abuse at the family's Palm Bay home. Melissa Doss (Brevard County Jail) A neighbor called police a day earlier to report that an unattended young girl had walked into his screened patio and could not communicate, according to an arrest report obtained by the Orlando Sentinel. When officers arrived at the scene, the child was able to show them where she lived and they went there to try to speak to her mother, police said.

The woman did not open the front door and, instead, jumped over a fence and walked around the house to speak with the officers, according to the report. Doss then told them her child had escaped without her knowledge, but she refused to let them go into her home, saying they would probably call the Florida

Department of Children and Families if they saw the inside of the house.

Wow! The state of people these day. They would rather let their child live with special needs, and torment them, rather than putting them in a home, or having an abortion? I do not support abortion, only if a person has been raped, or victim of incest without knowing it was unlawful. However, I also feel like if a child has extreme special needs where they can't learn nor live a normal lifestyle, they should also be put down, or supported by the family alone, and with love, nothing like the above case, where that child with autism had to endure such abuse to be locked in a cage as an animal. Notice how many of these cases include cages? They are stuck in captivity mode. It seems that they are stuck in slavery times, and still expect for everything to go accordingly to how their forefathers have lived. Thank YAH (GOD), I was raised by good parents that want the best for each of us. Here is the final case that I will speak on, for I do not need say more. Behind those doors.

Couple Who Tortured 12 Children in Their California Home Are Sentenced to Life – (Source: Wikipedia) *Louise Turpin and her husband, David Turpin, were sentenced to 25 years to life in prison for torturing 12 of their 13 children. Some of the children read statements at the hearing, detailing the years of abuse. Parents of 13 plead guilty to torture, abuse in case dubbed 'house of horrors'; David & Louise Turpin shackled, starved kids, kept some in cages.*

Though this be the last case I touch on, believe me when I say that these are not the only cases out there, which is a complete shame. To witness how some people are living out here, and may just live in a good area, with plenty of opportunities, and privileges, still end up committing such crimes, against others, as well as their own. This is roughly ten cases, while there is over one hundred plus cases in the search. I can't believe it when I read these cases, however, I knew such things would be going on across the world, knowing these are the ones within darkness that came to light, and have been exposed. Out of all the ones posted, I dislike the "Craigslist killer" the most, knowing he knew what he was doing was evil, and decided to kill himself upon being caught. It goes to show you that some people are so evil, and selfish out here, that they will get theirs, and not want to pay the price afterwards, just as those others had to endure. They will torment you, and keep you in bondage, but when it is their turn to burn per se, they want the easy way out, even claiming mental illness, and not guilty, due to the person not being able to free themselves, which is ignorant. Let me assure you that all of these sick bastards will pay, and will have to endure the same infliction that they inflicted upon others, towards themselves, when judgment day comes. For many will burn in the lake of fire for the evil that they have done unto others. There is not escaping judgment, and there is no escaping the second death.

I hope many more cases come out of the darkness, and those doing evil become exposed. Though we hope that there is no more cases as these ones mentioned, we would only be ignorant to not know that times have become worse, and to think this is not happening, would only be playing the fool. We are well aware that this is going on throughout the world, and even worse crimes than what these individuals had to committed. From little babies to adults, there are many vulnerable people out there in bondage, and being tormented, and tortured, while they were hoping for a normal life, there was one or more evil individuals that are selfish, and wanted to have their filthy fun, while using them as puppets. Such a shame, yet such a reality that we all must cope with, and witness, and for some, endure.

I would never want to live in those houses of these things happening in. I would not want to rent out any form of house that had such wickedness within, yet, behind those doors, there is a lot of smoke, and mirrors, and scenes that no one has witnessed. In truth, we all can be living in a place already that had such crimes being committed by others, and still, we will never know. There is a lot of paint on the walls, and nails in the floors, where you never know what you can expect to run into, live in, or even fall victim to, if you do not take care of yourself.

You have people working in ares of a career, even the government, police officers, and lawyers, and earthly judges, that are living in sin. Don't let the badges, nor medals, plaques, nor degrees fool you. They are human before all of that. They are sinners just like you and me. Notice we are born with a S.I.N. Number? For we are all born in sin, but it is up to us all to repent of sin, and walk uprightly. There are many that have so much dark secrets that is hid from the world, while they pretend to live righteous. There are so many perverted people that have on so much mask, that you will never find out about, until they get caught slipping up. Many in high seats tend to pay off people to hide their sin, or bride others. Behind those doors you will have parents that are not parents at all, but worthless pieces of shit that allow their kids, or should I say f*ck ups to do anything that they desire unto other people. They will never jump in to tell them to stop, nor repent. Instead, they will laugh, and encourage the more. The moment a real one ends up killing them, or beating the shit out of that joke of a child of theirs, that is when those so called "parents" start protesting on the news how their child was "so great", and "an angel". While the person who defends themselves, ends up having a terrible picture painted of them. Truth is, those called "parents" step up, only due to the fact that they do not want to be labelled as neglectful parents, and worthless. This happens ever so much, and it is much worse when the "parents" support much evil, compared to when the true parents, actually want to see an improvement within their out of control kid(s) who took the wrong path, away from their parents directions. For those who attempted to raise their children good, may be the ones who just ended up with terrible kids.

Behind those doors, only YAH (GOD) knows what is going on. We can only assume, and as many mind their own business, there may just be someone calling for help who needs you to mind their business for them. Regardless, the responsibility of each child, is their parents. The responsibility of each adult, is themselves. When all fails, you have no choice but to find assistance anywhere possible. Proving also that not everyone out here should have children. Not every women should give birth to children. Not every man should be able to have a relationship, nor the responsibility of children, for they are not classified as real men. Yet, how can you tell, and how can you judge, until evil, and wickedness is exposed.

As I'm on the topic of wickedness, beware of witches. Behind those doors, there are many that indulge in witchcraft, and sorcery. Many casting spells, voodoo, and all kinds of sorcery, even using dolls, and crystal balls, and even worse, using a stolen picture, or belongings that belonged to you. These heathen are so weak that they plot on the lives of others who may bring them discomfort, while telling it like it is. People hate the truth and when these witches are forced to hear the things that they do not like, they will not hesitate to cast any form of spell upon you. You may just be living in a place that devil witch doesn't like you living in, and she will do what she can to torment your living spaces. There is no limit to what people spend their time doing as they hide themselves behind walls/doors, and contemplate much sorcery, through self-hatred. I say "self-hatred because it starts with self. A person must really hate themselves to do such things that are so weak. They have no courage, nor bravery to face their enemies, instead they hide, and do the worst onto people that they can't even confront. Don't forget about time, for that is what they waste while having thoughts of you in the end. They have to visualize you, and conjure up spirits through the process, hoping that their traps, and plots work for them. This is going on ever to often behind doors, and it's a shame, for I believe all witches should get stoned to death.

<u>S C R I P T U R E</u>
EXODUS 22:18
KING JAMES VERSION

18 Thou shalt not suffer a witch to live.

<u>S C R I P T U R E</u>
LEVITICUS 20:7
KING JAMES VERSION

27 A man also or woman that hath a familiar spirit, or that is a wizard, shall surely be put to death: they shall stone them with stones: their blood shall be upon them.

Behind those doors, as soon as they close, you will never know who lives next door to you. You will never know the stranger that you met at a club, a bar, a library, or even a dating site.

You can only imagine, until you live with them that is. Going into the next chapter, relationships turned ugly.

CHAPTER
FIVE
UNTIL YOU LIVE
WITH THEM
(RELATIONSHIPS TURNED UGLY)

I will not mentions names, but since I have had the pleasure of living with females during dating stages, I have had a wide range of experience to know how women keep themselves. As I've had multiple female partners, even roommates, I can comfortably mention the experiences that I have had while living with females, due to not having a specific way of anyone feeling ashamed, nor singled out, nor accused, nor being that one, who many may know. Let me state the fact that living with females is a must for those who enter a relationship. Back in the day when there was morals, values, and order, and even strict discipline from parents, who taught their children to be clean, and to humble themselves, and even be modest women, have now thrown all of that out of the window, such teachings. In order for you to find a prize, you must sift through women as rice, and witness how they live, before making any form of commitment.

As pretty women can be on the outside, on the flesh, they should not automatically be complimented on the inside, for that is not the case for many, and many are not so beautiful. As I've mentioned, living with someone is more important than to just think you know someone based off of looks/conversation alone. There are people out here who shift change their mind and character often. This goes for men too, however, since I am a man, I will not express the ways of men, knowing I do not live with guys, and being straight, it would not be a good look on my end to speak upon them, aside from my own actions, being a man. Anyways, the reasoning that I say that you should live with a female before marriage (non-sexual), is due to the fact that they show you who they are while seeing them at all times. While having on make-up, and while that make-up comes off. I've been in a situation where there was a female that I never knew wore make-up, it was that good of an illusion, and then to find out, she had it on the whole time, until the next day it faded away, and she looked terrible. Having many blemishes and not looking anything as she used to. This individual made me take-aback firmly, and I had to re-adjust to this new look, hoping to have the same feelings towards her, but I couldn't. As I felt bad, that feeling went away, the moment I felt cheated to witness such a new face, compared to the face that I met. With that said, women, please be natural, and show a man what you look like without the glamour, and gold upon thy face, to prevent any form of disappointment on both ends.

A man should be flattered, and admire a woman's beauty that is natural. They should be happy with who you are in your natural stages. Even though love is more than skin deep, we as men deserve to witness the finished product, and not the confetti, covering up the prize. By doing so, you will only be appreciated more, and complimented for your natural self. There is no better feeling than to have someone want you for you, and not what you need to hide, and be ashamed of.

Now, aside from looks, let me touch on cleanliness. Guys, women are not as clean as they appear. As I've lived with many nationalities of women, most do not clean themselves properly when it comes to the flesh, and food. Many tend to not bathe/shower daily, and even take care of themselves during their monthly cycle. I've seen so much dirty pads, filth side up in the open trash can within the bathroom. And I mean, not even rolled up, but left open as well. The moment you go to use the bathroom, all you can smell is that stench. I've witnessed women using white towels while also going through such stages, with the dried up blood on the towel, and hung to dry. As bad as it may be for some guys that do not take care of themselves, while washing their behinds after taking a bowel movement, soiling their underwear, if not cleaned properly, and washed (you should be ashamed of yourselves), yes, women likewise do such things, and you will notice that, while laundry day or in clothes baskets. As I've learned to be clean, you must wash your butt after wiping, and lotion yourself after drying off from taking a stool. This way, you remain clean, and don't need to worry about ever having soiled underwear. If you are an adult, this should not be acceptable anywhere. I personally looked at certain females differently when I notice this area. You ain't sitting on my bed, nor am I going to be comfortable with you sitting on my couch. Ha ha. Shame.

Teeth are to be cleaned multiple times per day

as well. Scrubbing the tongue to prevent bad breath, helps as well. I don't know why but most females don't like brushing their teeth, nor scrubbing their tongue. I've witnessed females just wash their face with water, and not brush at all. Brushing up only takes a few minutes out of your day, and helps your teeth in the long run. You can also interact with people often, without them having to hold their breath. While speaking with you. When a person starts talking to you face to face, and looks at your mouth, aside from reading your lips, they most likely do not want any saliva catching on them from your mouth. Even in public, I missed heartbeats while talking to people, due to their stench of bad breath.

My point to this all is not to embarrass, but to help those who need to take care of themselves. Many people, men, and women, do not have someone to actually be honest, and upfront with them over such cases, due to being fake friends, or not wanting to embarrass their company kept. Aside from that, as I've been living with roommates that were all female, and of all nations, you must be careful of who you bring into your house. For your home is your sanctuary, and your body is your temple. What you allow into your life, and living space, is a dangerous thing. Before coming into the truth of my spirituality, and perfect religion. Matter of fact, in the process, while living with other nations, I actually began to take it much more serious based off of the interactions with roommates. The uncomfortable feeling of living with a female with statutes was something that I immediately regretted. I would tend to ask potential roommate prior to moving in, "what are your beliefs?", just to not get in conflict with my own, and to save time from having to have disagreements, and even ending up kicking them out. I like to be upfront, and when I lived with this one in particular, she lied, and was worshipping many elephants. She decorated her entire room with that stuff, even having an alter of some sort.

Now, as I rented out the room, I know what is in there room, is her own, however, it is still my own household, and that is what makes the difference. Her and I got along to an extent, however, she lied a lot, and was not clean as I thought she would be. On top of that, the statues were everywhere surrounding her belongings, and I am talking her knives, her spoons, and bowls within the shared kitchen. I couldn't have that surrounding me, and I had to request that she leaves, and so it was.

Honesty is important while living with people, for behind those doors, you never really know someone, unless they invite you in to knowing themselves. By being honest, to state the things that you like, compared to dislike, and what you believe, is important, just as much as you respect those you live with, and their rules. Without complying, it will only end bad, and on ugly terms. For her, she left peacefully, and there was no drama thereafter. From that point on, I made specific contracts that they would sign, just to secure my end, and being able to make it possible to get rid of individuals that didn't comply with my demands from the gate.

There is nothing better than to live with people of the same background, and understanding. Finding someone with similar intentions is a good thing. My mind state was, get money, live in peace, and have a clean environment to live in, while being comfortable around one another. What you do outside the house, I could care less, but just as long as you do not bring that drama back to my house. For I have to live here.

Those that live next to you, again of which I do not considered neighbours. I would recommend not forcing a friendship, nor any form of communication, other than basic greetings. This is only good for the sake of peace, and easy approaching purposes Most people that live close by, only want to know your business, and want to get "close", in order to invade your privacy. The more open they become, the more the question come as well, to the point, where you are in too deep. Notice the questions are typically one-sided? It is due to the fact that people only want to know about you, and not give out too much about themselves, or maybe it is because you just don't care to ask about those things, as much as they inquire about those things against you? A primes example, someone asking, "what do you do for a living?". It's basic, "I'm surviving". Anything that I do, is surviving, for we are living in a concrete jungle, and we must do whatsoever we must do to survive.   The same reason I never ask that question first, knowing it's none of my business, and most people feel uncomfortable telling their business out, due to not in a career that they actually want to be in. In most cases, people tend to volunteer while telling me their business.

When it comes to relationships, again, it is all about trials and errors. We never know who we will end up with, until we are inside one another space. You need to take the time to want to be in that relationship, and it's important to not force anything that is not there. People will become trapped when they take this step too serious. When I say, "too serious", is when you invest a bit too much money, and time, when you do not think it will work out. Just let that situation die off, and do not hold one another hostage. I can recall a time when there was a female that I was dating, and her, and I would bump heads. I could not tolerate the ways of her lifestyle, and I could not see it long term. So, I ended it, however, she became sour, and instead of staying on course for self, which was make money, and live in peace, she started to bring drama, and unnecessary attention, knowing she was the toxic one. It got to the point where distractions were everywhere, taking away form the initial agreement. Such a shame, but still a learning.

Do not live with women that like you, and are attracted to you. This is dangerous on many levels, and I learned this first hand. As I used to have roommates in my younger years, I preferred to live with females, as I am a straight man, and don't like to wake up daily to another guy that is not blood, being family within the household. Although separate rooms, it is awkward and should not be done for mature men, as myself. If sharing a full house with two too three, that is different, and to each his own. I was living with a female that wanted to be with me, and this situation turned ugly fast, knowing I didn't feel the same way. As she tried to make her move on me, she then became embarrassed knowing I rejected her. As she wanted to then turn sour against me, it began to mess up my time, and money, which is something I was trying to take advantage of. When she turned ugly on me, she ruined the business venture. Now, though this is common to happen, knowing people of opposite sex attract, however, when one side of the agreement goes sour, the whole thing falls down. Which brings me to the next topic of money.

Money relationships is something that you need to part ways with when it comes to family, and friends. Try your best to never put money between your relationships of so. Money ruins a lot of people's relationships, and can be the focal point in all relationships. Business needs to be separate from family and friends. For when time comes to money, you need to not involve sympathy, nor emotions. It should be blunt, and to the point. As I work part time, I go to work, and make sure it's all about work. I aim to not keep personal conversation too often, knowing I am not there for that, but to make my ends meet, and so, I leave exactly when my time is done, without sticking around to have conversations, for time is money, and money is on time. All things therein must be held on the clock, and not off the time. When it comes to doing business with family, which is good to break bread with your own, however, I would rather just share my gains with family, and friends by holding feast days, or treating everyone to something, rather than trying to get something together through splitting. You wouldn't want to live with family, and have money issues, for you will only lose that bond, and have many sleepless nights, due to bickering, and disagreements, that can turn sour quickly.

My best advice, is keep friends and family away from money topics. You will lose so much time, over money, and it is typically petty situations that will not turn out good, nor in your favour. Family is meant to be there for one another, likewise with friendships. You should keep it there. As for relationships, do not jump into living with anyone, until you are invested in time to figure out as much as possible. Do not make it a huge jump to where you will end up losing more than you should. It's best to take your time, and meet that right person, while gradually moving in together, but know what your intentions are on the same page as one another. Nothing forced, nor puffed up. Beware of shape-shifters that may be chameleons. For once you live with them, behind those doors, everything will change for the worst.

CHAPTER
SIX
TOO MANY
CHAMELEONS
(SHAPE SHIFTERS)

It seems like in this day and age, we are dealing with so many people that are deceptive, and appear so fake. Their ways are not true. Their promises and not sincere. Their words are shallow and have no dept of truth within it. Many people in this world of ours are sellouts, and followers, rather than leaders. As we live in a society of lies, and the majority of people are so two-face chameleons, you can't trust anybody, nor feel comfortable allowing someone to gain your trust. If they do not live under the same roof as yourself, you will never know how that person truly is. Most people expose themselves before you even give them the opportunity to prove themselves worthy. Your word is everything, and when you see people shifting often, and even supporting the ways of fake, it is troubling. It's like someone giving you their word, and then when you hold them to it, they change up their stance, and begin to deny it, as well as support it, so that you come off as the liar.

There are many people in this world that are mask wearers, and have many mask that they change into often, depending on the place.

Now, as I used to work retail, including sales for a short period of time. I noticed the persona that I had to put on to make sales, according to the ways of the business. I hated it so much, but needed the money at the time, and wanted to do my best regardless. Working at a young age, I felt like this role was terrible for the fact, I would put on the smile, and be nice to people, while trying to push a product that is not even something that I care about. As for the people, I would not talk to just anyone, but knowing it was apart of the job, I made myself comfortable. It began to come off as a script, and I never enjoyed that role, for when I left the location of the company, and my shift was over, while heading back home, when I would get a call, or meet up with someone, it was as if I was brainwashed, and talking the same way with the people I knew. Example, (script) "Hi, how are you today, can I offer you assistance with your shopping?", while having a fake smile on, and knowing how it would feel as if I was that customer, instead I was as that robot, and when I would get off the shift, I would still have that feeling to talking in the same tone, and manner. Again, this was in the early stages of work when I did retail, during my early 20's.

I've never stepped back into sales again after that one job due to feeling like a robotic person that was no where close to who I am. That is a light example, for there are people out here that stay in those realms, and behave the same way, without getting paid to do so. They will talk nice to you, while outside, but when you see them again, they change who they are. Sometimes even while in different settings, and while with other people surrounding them. As I put myself first, I know what I am talking about, and have changed from such ways. I stay away from places that require for you to "put on", instead of "**BE YOU**" attitude. Don't let money make you do things out of pocket. As an author, and music producer, I continue to promote my information, and products, but do so genuine, where apart of me is not being sold, but shared with the customers.

The worst cases are when you meet someone that appears genuine, and you bond/vibe with them. The next time you see them, they pretend like you do not even exist. As they behave as if they never knew you, nor had a conversation with you at all before. And it can be a couple days that separates that time frame of last seeing them. If that is what it is, let it be so for good, and do not come back around thinking we are on good terms, or have that access, for I would feel crossed already, and look on you as crazy.

I can't stand kiss-ass people. Those who laugh along with you, when things are not funny. Yet, they laugh, just to make you feel good. Likewise when they are your co-workers that you thought were real, but when they are next to their supervisor or boss, they start kissing ass, and being "yes men". I believe in treating everyone the same. Yes, I know that you can't be as open with certain people who may be in position, however, that doesn't stop you from keeping your same morals, and values, as well as being true to self. There has never been a time that I kissed ass of anyone that was in power. There is one thing to be nice, and to not embarrass, but to actually go out of your way, trying to please your boss or supervisor, will not be something I would ever do. As a hard worker, I worked, while I know my worth, and know that I bring something to the table, without looking for a handout. As I push my own weight, and have a value, I know that it's a fair exchange enough. Those who kiss ass tend to lack in many areas, and rely upon the one-sided effect, which is kissing ass to feel nice enough not to get fired/laid off, as well as obtain favour for promotions. People keep forgetting that you have one life to live. Being real is always going to make you sleep better at night. You are not promised the second life, if you do not repent, and live in a good way during this life of ours. We do not have to kiss-ass nor be fake with anyone. We can be bold, but still be respectful. We can always speak our mind, for what purpose would it be, if we do not be ourselves at all times?

Now, people that hate themselves, tend to spend more time on other people, in the negative. The more they tend unto others in the negative, the more they hide themselves from facing their own reality. They will pry into your business, while not sharing anything about themselves, other than displaying victimized personalities, and sorrow. They feel as the world owes them something for being failures. As if failing is not normal and deserves a price. When people hate themselves, they don't mind being in a position where they feel like they are perfect, which is false. They are comfortable lying to themselves, hoping to believe their false life, and usually are the ones to act as if they are the best person to ask for opinions, even on situations that never concerned them. First to speak as if they are established and been down that road before. Always experienced with nothing to show, nor prove any of it. There is nothing worse than having someone comment on something that you never asked their opinion on, and to have that same person who has never been down that road before, pretend to know the curves of the street. It's pointless.

We all once lives next to someone who is trying to pretend to own everything. That same person who doesn't belong speaking on anything concerning you, nor anyone else. That person wants to behave controlling, and will go out of their way to try and get as much information as possible. They will try to befriend you, and often times try to jab at you in the process. They will try to take steps in your life, and what I mean by that is, today they will ask you about yourself, tomorrow, they will ask about who is behind your doors.

The next day, they will ask, how much money you make, and try to get as much information as possible. When that fails, and you call the person out on their bullshit, that person will never fight their own battles, but create strife between others and you, while using the simple-minded to not think, but do on his/her behalf, just to get his/her way. Again, I hate picking on any nation of people, but I will call it for what it is, and say, Caucasians are the type of people that do this often. I know this by experience, and not just off of word of mouth, although I've heard the same things likewise from others.

They are people I try my best to not have small talk with at all. I ignore, or keep it to the minimum with "hi", and "bye". I don't like their ways, and would never choose to live next door to them. As they are the biggest chameleons on this planet, I would rather live among the ignorant, and simple-minded that at least keep it real. I'm not trying to stir up strife, but to only express the truth the best way I know how, and to relate everything possible to matters that concerned me most, against people that have been against me most, and it is not my own people, but that nation of people, and that nation being the Edomite nation (Caucasians).

I look at situations that one may have to face. And I look at those responsible, and involved in the situations, while they will do everything possible, to destroy what you have built, and burn your trail of reaching higher limits. Once they do this to you, they go on with their lives as nothing happened. Not caring about the damage that they have caused. We all need to eat and everyone does the same things ultimately, when it comes to the basics. We all go grocery shopping, while needing food to survive. We all use the bathroom. We all need to maintain our lives, no matter how it may be. The truth behind it is, those who harm others lives, don't understand the basics can be altering ones life drastically. For this cause, it is better to not harm the lives of others existence, without thoroughly having harmful intentions that will never come back your way, for once you create that enemy, you will become a target.

A good teacher is one who tells you to remain

the same always. I learned from the best teacher possible, and with that said, I've always been happy with myself, my actions, and my personality. There has not been a time that I felt "fake", or "not being true", knowing I would feel it right away. And so, I keep it 100% always, and will always be true. I am happy to know that who I am today, I will be tomorrow, but only changed for the better, more renewed, more brighter, smarter/wiser, and in better spirit. So, when you see me a year from now, don't expect for me to change who I am. Do not expect for me to change who I am for the worse, whether money is in my pocket, or not, the same person with the same personality, is who I will be, knowing I am comfortable with all that I am. As I am indoors, I am outdoor.

<u>S C R I P T U R E</u>
HEBREWS 13:8
KING JAMES VERSION

8 Jesus Christ the same yesterday, and to day, and for ever.

CHAPTER
SEVEN
UGLINESS STARTS FROM WITHIN SELF
(BE NOT DECEIVED)

As I've grown older, and become wiser, through trials, and tribulations, as well as experience through the burning, learning however which way that I can, I've noticed that beauty is more than skin deep. We must look towards the inside of individuals in order to find out who we are actually in conversation with, through any form of relationships. There are people out there that are someone evil inside their home, while they come off kind, and tender while outside, and then showing a whole new character which is masking. These type of people are pretenders, and typically can be as gothic, while inside, dark, wicked, and then outside wearing a crucifix. I do not know why they chose to do such things, for they are only fooling themselves. Those who have an eye for good and evil, know who is who just based off looks, speech patterns, before even any form of actions. In most cases those righteous judgments become true. As I have came across such people often, I noticed that they wear the crucifix to appear holy, and nice, while they are inwardly deceivers. As written in the most recent chapter "Too many chameleons", these people are shape-sifters.

People   show a lot of what they are on the outside, that rarely matches what is on the inside. What is the outside? The outside is the flesh. The flesh and the worldly materialistic things that many form upon themselves, as well as, the surrounding things that accompany them, like their car, their home, and their attire. The outside also symbolizes their mask that they tend to put on, while displaying for the whole world. What is the inside? Well, that is the brain, the heart, the spirit, the soul. The personality that is the persona that one displays. The eyes are the key to the soul, and I believe that is true. For many people have eyes that tell a story about themselves, while others have eyes that are deceiving, and full of mischief.

The eyes of one who has the stare of comeliness, and humble, yet bright, and welcoming, tend to have a personality on the inside that matches their outside. Being honest, reliable, faithful, and sincere. Those who have a cold stare, as if there is no one there, or is dark, they have a inside that is filled with mischief, and evil. They can't be trusted. While you have those who have that half smile eyes, where they squint often, and show you that you can be deceived, if you fall into temptation of the lust of the eyes.

<u>SCRIPTURE</u>
PSALM 36:2
KING JAMES VERSION

2 For he flattereth himself in his own eyes,
until his iniquity be found to be hateful.

Then you have the eyes of darkness, and those people are pure evil, while showing you who they are on the outside as well. Which type of eyes do you have? I look in the mirror, and know that my eyes tell a story. The pain and long-suffering, while showing sincerity is natural, and as it matches my inside, I will be on that walk in truth. Many also recognize my eyes, while they compliment me, and even tell me that they can tell by my eyes, the kind of man that I am. As they can find some form of trust in me. They know that I am sincere, as well as someone who will help them.

How someone looks you in the eyes, they show you that they are not afraid, and do show respect. Shifty eyes are always going to be liars. Look everyone in their face, even the enemy. For there is people out there just waiting to test you.

S C R I P T U R E
JEREMIAH 1:8
KING JAMES VERSION

8 Be not afraid of their faces: for I am with thee to deliver thee, saith the LORD.

Am a man that likes wearing shades. I like to protect my eyes, whoever I am not afraid to show my eyes. Many people that wear shades indoors, usually have terrible spirits. They are evil, and shady. Lately I've been witnessing most people with shifty eyes, and deceiving eyes. Those that you cannot trust. Trust no man, but always move accordingly, while moving on intuition. Once you can understand how someone is, you can cope more in life easier. Not that it is good to judge, however, if you are blessed to know the difference, as I am, you can tell people's character faster, and from that point on, you can give access to your life, or refrain them from entering, and going further.

I think about hate, and measure it to haters. Haters are going to be ones who always are jealous, envious, and bitter towards the lives of others. While those who hate, tend to just be cold, yet brutally honest, and don't care to get in contact with you. It's a mutual understanding of separation and avoiding one another, by any means necessary. When you hate someone, you do not like seeing them, nor hearing their voice, nor being close to them at any time. Compared to haters, who actually admire your life, and want to be closer to you. Most people that hate others, and want to be close, may just be jealous, but tend to have hate for themselves. They hate who they are and their existence is bitter, knowing they want for you to feel pain, and lose in life, only to be as themselves. As we live within this era of materialistic living, and technology, we are witnessing a lot of self hate that is going on. Many are exposing themselves as haters, that hate who they are, and do not want to live in truth, and reality. Instead, they want to live a lie, while ignoring the facts of life.

The number one rule to self, is to love self. Many do not know love, yet they have nothing but hate for who they are, and hide behind so much distractions that this world has to offer, even substances that alter their mind, and actions, through drugs, and liquor. As life goes on, they move further away from who they are, and adapt to the ways of others. This is the cause for many followers. For even fools have followers of many. As they following trends, they continue to expose themselves as lost individuals. Whether it be music trends, or clothing/fashion trends, their ways are always altering, and moving with the times.

I look at "Hip Hop". It has many decades of changing. From tight jeans, too baggy jeans, and then to no belt jeans, while they exposing their underwear. Then, now to extremely tight jeans, while still exposing their ass. It's like generations have been mixed up, and blended together to create the worst of them all. As we can see now, from crooked, many have turned straight, and are wearing regular jeans today, or even shorts. My point to it all is, people change who they are typically due to the persuading of others. Being followers of man. I encourage everyone out there to be themselves, and stop going with the flow of things. As they that do so, will only expose how their character is, and how insecure they truly are. I stand proud to say that I found myself at an early age, and was never one to go with the flow of man. I never followed the fashion trend, and as I have changed what I listen to by subtracting toxic lyrics/words that have no purpose in my life today. I am in control of my own actions, and what I allow into my life. Though the people in this world who are sinful, tend to try and dictate all that others should do, while promoting themselves, and their way as the only acceptable way. Who are you that I should follow?

Now, I want to touch on how evil people that are behind walls/doors. There are so much people that have wicked ways, and bad, evil intentions. They are toxic to this world, and behind those doors, they expose the most out of themselves. I think about how people in this world can truly hide behind doors, and do such things that are unimaginable. For example, the fact that there are many racist within this world, and as you may live right next door to some, you may also work with some, and even have them within your family.

When you think about racism, where does that stem from? Of course within self. It has to be from emotions, and fear, as well as, a form of hate/prejudice that is generated towards another nation of people. While racism is on the rise, we the more the people will continue to create that hate within their homes. Even if that means supporting what they represent within themselves, such as pictures of racism symbolic signs, and so on. I look at the KKK, and how they live their lives. It starts from within. They have hate within themselves, which also generates hate, but through fear. The reason fear is there, is due to the fact that the hide who they are in the public eye, compared to groups like "The Black Panther Party", who wear their clothing in public, while supporting the push for Black unity, and the power within. Never have they hid who they are, nor what they represent. They walk boldly, and do not cover up a thing. Compared to these KKK members who work in law offices, police force, and other sectors that would only spark outrage.

I look at my fringes, and I wear them everywhere as well. From inside my house, to outdoors, and even work, while working for other nations. I am not afraid of who I am. I am not afraid to represent what I believe in. I know why I wear those fringes, and it is not to show that I am racist, nor hateful towards anyone. I do this not for show, but for the sake of my YAH (GOD), giving me the laws, statutes, and commandments to wear these fringes with the ribbon of blue, throughout my generations. As an Israelites, I am keeping the commandments, and abiding by the rules set before me, and with that said, it is there for me to repent of my sin, compared to commit any sin against another. For it is designed to protect self from committing sin. See Number 15:38-41 (KJV).

When I was younger I would look towards the flesh of a woman rather than anything else. I would even date them, and tolerate the things I disliked about them, just to please the flesh. Then, once older, knowing how much the flesh is deceiving, and troublesome, it is best to always seek out the insides. The flesh will never last, especially as you age. For some nations, worse than others, however, I am not here to be ignorant, but to speak in truth. And every nation of people, the flesh will perish, and wrinkle, not look the same as it sued to, once young. So, seek the things that always remain the same. The heart, and mind will be there, and once you rise in love with those features, it will last much longer than the flesh, I assure you. Don't be as those who get caught up with the flesh and fall into temptation, while their destiny is the pit. Many men allow the flesh to lead them, and the flesh is a mask already, so do what is smart, and be true.

<u>S C R I P T U R E</u>
REVELATION 2:20-23
KING JAMES VERSION

20 Notwithstanding I have a few things against thee, because thou sufferest that woman Jezebel, which calleth herself a prophetess, to teach and to seduce my servants to commit fornication, and to eat things sacrificed unto idols.

21 And I gave her space to repent of her fornication; and she repented not.

22 Behold, I will cast her into a bed, and them that commit adultery with her into great tribulation, except they repent of their deeds.

23 And I will kill her children with death and all

the churches shall know that I am he which searcheth the reins and hearts: and I will give unto every one of you according to your works.

CHAPTER
EIGHT
BETTER TO ABIDE ALONE
(PEACE BEHIND THESE DOORS)

<u>S C R I P T U R E</u>
1 CORINTHIANS 7:8
KING JAMES VERSION

8 I say therefore to the unmarried and widows, it is good for them if they abide even as I.

Alone may be scary for a lot of people out here in this cold world. For women it should be more a concern than for men. Knowing women need strength surrounding them during their older years. There is nothing worse than witnessing an elderly woman that has no children, no husband, and nor support. Out in this world to live for self, and do for self, with no one even caring to support her. Even if she were to eventually go into a elderly nursing home, she may just get taken advantage of and mistreated. For that same reason, I would never do such things unto my parents, for that is not honouring your parents, but casting them away.

Now, we must all know that women are less than men on this planet, not in numbers but in strength. Most have put themselves in that position while displaying themselves are unattractive, and polluted. Many women have also been playing the game of "hard to get", and now that they have grown older, it has turned upon them where the getting gets harder. No one looks at them the same, and they think that they still have it, but don't. The feeling that someone "owes you something", is foolish to believe, and you will not get very far. The worst kind of woman, is the type to think that she is above all, including you.

As I mentioned elderly women, though the sight is hard to witness when you see them old, and having no love, nor support, it makes me briefly sad, and then I remember the days that we are living in today. I can't feel sorry for women when they are not offering true values towards decent men. Many are overstepping their boundaries, while trying to be the head of the household, and the pants wearers. Men then become annoyed with the constant battles, and annoying behaviours that these women display, only go astray. They feel like their privates have a higher value than men parts, and believe men, even married men should fight, beg, and fuss for opportunities to lay with them. I could understand those who are not married, but those that are married, they need to be more available onto their husband, instead of behaving as if they have a turn off switch when they reach the stages of marriage. Aside from that, most women are behaving as if you should put her first before everything, including your beliefs, your parents, and your values. As if you should give them up, and put her before all, or else she will threaten to leave. Well, let her go, because she needs to play her role.

S C R I P T U R E
PROVERB 21:9
KING JAMES VERSION

9 It is better to dwell in a corner of the housetop, than with a brawling woman in a wide house.

As a single man, I can tell you that it is much better to abide alone. I've had my fair share of relationships, and if you can't compromise nor have a complete understanding of agreements on all major things, life will be a headache. Life will never be peaceful, which is something all men with purpose seek. I do not have to do anything that I do not want to do. I go where I want to go, and am more happy alone. If it were all about intercourse, I would be more on the side of wanting to be with someone, however, when you get older, your mind looks at that as only a benefit, and special, if you were to share it with one true women, especially to avoid fornication.

<u>S C R I P T U R E</u>
1 CORINTHIANS 7:2
KING JAMES VERSION

2 Nevertheless, to avoid fornication, let every man have his own wife, and let every woman have her own husband.

Now, do not let me tell you that being alone is always going to be a good thing, even for men. Having someone by your side who is helps meet, is a good thing. Someone who compliments your lifestyle, and has the same vision, and lifestyle, and goals. Even to bear your children. For me, it was just hard to find someone who has similar qualities, and to find that, takes a lot of effort, which I no longer have the patience for. You have to get to know someone, while putting in so much time, and effort. Money wasted on dates, and then as you get past the "fake stages", which is typically that female showing me all that she is not, until she gets comfortable enough to expose her true self, unleashing that mask, while behind the doors. That takes time, and time is nothing to waste. And people tend to change. Behind those doors, she will be someone totally different, and that to me is a long process.

You don't want to be in a relationship, that may have been marriage, just to feel like you have baggage with you. That is the worst. I've seen so many relationships/marriages that have been held together due to a child, and/or just because. The couple are not happy at all, but miserable and wasting time. Why hang onto something that is not there? Why force something, and live bitter, while in anger? Some have children, and use that child as a reason to hang on, while not giving that child the life that he/she deserves. Some people I've noticed do not compliment one another, but are each others thorn, and downfall. Why? If you have to live like that, and it comes to that point where you are just living together, and unhappy, you are only fooling yourselves, and holding something together that is already broken.

Again, to be honest, if you can find that mate, you will be better off, while having all the perks life can offer any couple. You can share your burdens, and have someone that will always have your back, front, and sides. Being able to erase any form of loneliness, as well as creating such memories that is best to be shared with another, being a partner/spouse. On top of all that goodness, you can form together and create babies. Your genes get to be spread. Nothing like getting the opportunity to see what your son or daughter will look like. It's even better to know that as a strong couple, you can raise your child in any form of way that suits yourselves. Being able to train up a child to be the best that he/she can be, is a blessing, but only when trained to be positive.

As I touch on the topic of children, allow me to now talk about how things can go sour if you have the wrong spouse, and have children together. The first thing that I wanted to touch on is the fact that, if you are not of the same culture, it will surely be a struggle raising your child. When it comes to beliefs, you will eventually ignore them if your spouse believes in something totally different, due to culture differences, and nationalities. I can relate to this as when I was younger and seeking truth within my religion, I ended up meeting a girl that looked very attractive and we related on many levels, however, the difference is, that we never served the same beliefs. For mine, I believed, and know that my YAHH (GOD), HE is King of kings, LORD of lords, and GOD of gods. The Alpha and Omega, the beginning and the ending.

<u>S C R I P T U R E</u>
REVELATION 22:13
KING JAMES VERSION

13 I am Alpha and Omega, the beginning and the end, the first and the last.

Now, knowing that, I didn't care to know about her religion nor her beliefs as I will never inquire to care, knowing I know in my heart that the true YAH (GOD) is the YAH (GOD) of Abraham, Isaac, and Jacob, the YAH (GOD) of Israel, above all. So, automatically I know that she was not the one for me, and had to set myself free. Now, as I knew I had attraction for her, I knew I must put my faith before her, or else I would not be a true believer. Many people tend to bypass the fact that your true walk is important, and if you are an Israelite as I am, that is a believer in the Holy Bible, you will certainly follow the laws, statues, and commandments that are set before us, especially if we read the Scripture. For those who know to do good, and doeth it not, to him it is sin.

<u>S C R I P T U R E</u>
JAMES 4:17
KING JAMES VERSION

17 Therefore to him that knoweth to do good,
and doeth it not, to him it is sin.

The reasoning we had to end it, was due to the fact that if I were to continue with her, I would be ignoring all that I know, and choosing her over my YAH (GOD). For if you read the Holy Bible, it shows you that you should stay within your own, and by living with that heathen, I would reject my YAH (GOD), and in the end, HE will reject me.

<u>S C R I P T U R E</u>
2 CORINTHIANS 6:17
KING JAMES VERSION

17 Wherefore come out from among them, and
be ye separate, saith the Lord, and touch not

the unclean thing; and I will receive you.

SCRIPTURE
1 CORINTHIANS 7:32-33
KING JAMES VERSION

32 But I would have you without carefulness. He that is unmarried careth for the things that belong to the Lord, how he may please the Lord:

33 But he that is married careth for the things that are of the world, how he may please his wife.

SCRIPTURE
MATTHEW 10:33
KING JAMES VERSION

33 But whosoever shall deny me before men, him will I also deny before my Father which is in Heaven.

The worst would be to lose the connection of the Creator, however, what if things were to go bad down the line between the two of you within the relationship? What if I never got along with her later, and we departed ways, how would it feel to then go back to studying? Wouldn't I be a sellout, and already a traitor? What if you end up having a child together with a heathen from another nation? Then, that makes it different, for you must not have known your true beliefs while marrying a heathen, and having children together, which is a pass, and you will not be held accountable, ONLY if you did not know. Again, to him that knoweth to do good. If you did not know, then you can't be held accountable, but if you did, you will be judged.

No one should confuse their own children to believe in half and half. For none can serve to masters, and if you do not have the same god, then you are not serving the same entirely, and truthfully. I can't image having a Bible study with a group of fellow believers to have my wife sitting there in her attire, and having statues around the place, while studying her religion. It would only make the people question me, and before that, I would have no choice but to feel awkward, knowing I first would come to understanding that "this is not right".

Aside from beliefs, you now must know the rules to raising a child, and if you have a partner that may just be facing divorce, and may already have another partner by her side, who is set to take over your role, while with your soon to be ex-wife. How will you handle the fact that they may just raise your child differently from your own standards? For if you get split custody, you then raise your child on certain days, and your ex, as well as her new partner, decides to raise your child a different way. Although your ex is put away, and should not be able to mingle with other men, knowing she is bound to you, however, your beliefs are your end, they do not keep it up, nor uphold those same laws the same. All of this sounds like confusion, and this is why it is best to take your time when finding a mate. Make it simple keeping your beliefs, and structure firm in all that you do. It goes the same for a non-believers, for that person will only eventually choose what ever beliefs that they desire later on, and then it can get even worse. Speaking on confusion, imagine if you were deep into marriage, and married to a heathen with many kids, while upholding her beliefs, and then coming into the truth, what would you do then? It is only logic to be the head, and make sure all those with you, (wife and children) abide by your beliefs, or depart from her, while giving a letter of divorcement. Remember, before man, before woman, before mother, before father, is the Most High. So, coming into the truth, the truth will still be the truth, and that is what you should follow.

The reason I state that being alone is best, is to avoid such situations, knowing those who believe in what I believe in, is hard to come by, especially where I live. For me, it will be extra harder finding a perfect mate, however, well worth the wait if that female would come to pass, knowing she would have all the qualities that I am looking for, and receive in return a good man in me. This is apart of living for YAH (GOD), and not for self. As I continue to keep that same structure, I can do no wrong. For those who are not taking beliefs serious, without any proper foundation, you will not be happy, and it will only go sour later in life if you decide to take on religious beliefs of others. Not aiming that having beliefs are a bad thing, but it is more of a structure, and firm foundation that can lead one to better days if you are in the true gospel.

Peace is something one must find in order to

feel at best. Peace is what makes days go by easier, and there is many areas of "peace" that one must seek. First being peace of mind, which I believe is the most important form of peace. For it can give you clarity at all times, and at all places. The second form of peace, is peace in surroundings. If your surrounding is filled with chaos, loud noise, and drama, no matter how sound your mind is, you will lose concentration, and only live in rage, and discomfort. Find peace and comfort within yourself. Be true.

CHAPTER
NINE
BE TRUE

SCRIPTURE
DEUTERONOMY 28:6
KING JAMES VERSION

6 Blessed shalt thou be when thou comest in, and blessed shalt thou be when thou goest out.

Be true. Whether you are behind the doors, or outside in the general public, be true to self, and be true to the truth. We have so much fakes in this world, so many deceivers, so many pretending, and so many living a lie, that people are become more, and more unattractive. Humans are become more than cancers to this earth, to the point this world is being destroyed by man. They seek a new place to call home in the sky due to not wanting to face responsibility. Hoping to escape the mess that they created. The vain lifestyles, the chasing of money, while exposing themselves as worthless in the process, even sellouts. There are also those who try to overpower, and become gods on earth. Many has become the same, and the majority are doing such things while looking so disgusting in the process. What people will do for money? What people would do for attention? What people will do just to fit in?

What people will do to get their way? What people will do to obtain power, and control? How much land does one man need? All of which things that only show how worthless, perverted, selfish, greedy, and ignorant they can be, and it is a total shame.

For me, I hate fake people. I hate people that are nothing real. They live a lie, and the truth is behind those doors. Yet, not everyone has access to behind those doors, nor should anyone really need access to figure out true people, from fake people, for real recognize real, while fake get exposed due to their own words, and actions that are not sincere. I look at Caucasians for example, and witness such evidence that they are evil, by posting videos of themselves doing such things against other nations of people, such as us Blacks (Israelites). Such as I have written also about themselves doing wickedness, even unto their own family members. Stating how much they hate our kind, and how worthless we are, alongside bywords, and relating to us as animals, while hiding. They show how weak they are in their attempts, knowing they are more comfortable doing such things in darkness per say, rather than in our faces. Same reason the KKK members wear mask, instead of being bold to expose who they are. As they work for companies, they do not want to jeopardize their position. As an author, who is not afraid to speak my mind, I am comfortable telling it like it is, knowing I speak truth, and can back it up with not only actions but examples of evidence of all that these heathens do unto my people, as well as myself. See many of my books to get better understanding of how real I keep it. Make every man be held accountable for his words and actions, and so I will be confident in my own.

Be true to yourself, while allowing your first home, being your temple, your body, which should be the best place to display. While taking care of your mind, body, and soul, you should always preserve life, and respect thyself. Do not corrupt your soul, by tainting your body. If you are one to put marks upon your skin (tattoos), and indulge in a lot of eating of bad foods, as well as taking drugs, and going a whoring, it can certainly expose your home to the point, no one would want you, nor to even see how you are living beyond your body. Pray often, and when you go to pray, make your temple clean by praying even inside of a closet within your home to keep the privacy of your prayer between you and the Most High.

S C R I P T U R E
MATTHEW 6:6
KING JAMES VERSION

6 But thou, when thou prayest, enter into thy closet, and when thou hast shut thy door, pray to thy Father which is in secret; and thy Father which seeth in secret shall reward thee openly.

We as Israelites (Blacks, Negroes, and African Americans) need to understand what " being true" really means. We are different from the rest, and should never live the ways that these heathen live, for we are chosen, and must live the way our Heavenly Father, the Most High wants us to live, while keeping HIS laws, statutes, and commandments. As the world changes, we must remain true. As you can witness what is going on with the world today, with this gay agenda going on. We do not need to turn gay to survive, nor fit in. We do not need to be weak men, nor feminine /

effeminate to dress as they dress, and be weaker in muscle mass, just to be apart of the progress of the land. We must be strong, and through long-suffering, use our strength gained through that suffering as a benefit in life, while not partaking in their wicked way. We are made different, and need to respect ourselves, while not caring for what other people think about us.

SCRIPTURE
REVELATION 3:8
KING JAMES VERSION

8 I know thy works: behold, I have set before thee an open door, and no man can shut it: for thou hast a little strength, and hast kept my word, and hast not denied my name.

As the world is pushing for women to be empowered, we will not submit ourselves to be less than they, while allowing them to run the household. We know our role, and will be bold men, while our women repent, and keep order.

SCRIPTURE
1 CORINTHIANS 11:3-10
KING JAMES VERSION

3 But I would have you know, that the head of

every man is Christ; and the head of the woman is the man; and the head of Christ is God.

4 Every man praying or prophesying, having his head covered, dishonoureth his head.

5 But every woman that prayeth or prophesieth with her head uncovered dishonoureth her head: for that is even all one as if she were shaven.

6 For if the woman be not covered, let her also be shorn: but if it be a shame for a woman to be shorn or shaven, let her be covered.

7 For a man indeed ought not to cover his head, forasmuch as he is the image and glory of God: but the woman is the glory of the man.

8 For the man is not of the woman: but the woman of the man.

9 Neither was the man created for the woman; but the woman for the man.

10 For this cause ought the woman to have power on her head because of the angels.

As this world keeps going into a new age of technology and programming, we need to not use it to become weak, nor robots. As they make robotic women dolls with all the features of a woman, who many evil nations have used to replace the natural woman, we will not comply, nor be so lonely and pathetic that we take that route at all. Instead, we will wait upon the LORD for our prize wives, and repent of fornication, and adultery. As this world keeps going on, and the ways of man become more and more wicked, while they hide behind their doors, and even bring those filthy imaginations to reality, we must not care for them to learn, nor to take on their customs. We should never want to bring into our homes such wicked devices, and should keep ourselves clean. For what we bring into our houses, may be our own destruction.

<u>S C R I P T U R E</u>
JEREMIAH 10:2
KING JAMES VERSION

2 Thus saith the LORD, learn not the way of the way of the heathen, and be not dismayed at the signs of heaven; for the heathen are dismayed at them.

As I write my books for the Israelites (Blacks, Negroes, African Americans), although all can read, and support, I gear my books towards my own people, and so that our people wake up to the truth, as well as repent of sin, while doing the will of our Father, who Art in Heaven. We must take heed to wisdom and obtain the understanding that is required to survive in this world. I do not know many Israelites out here in the world, however, I am that I am, and opened my door to you so that you can learn and be wise. I open my door to you so that I can lead by example, just as the Messiah, Christ, who showed us the way, we must all do likewise.

SCRIPTURE
REVELATION 3:20
KING JAMES VERSION

20 Behold, I stand at the door, and knock: if any man hear my voice, and open the door, I will come in to him, and will sup with him, and he with me.

With love and peace, may the people be blessed and keep repentance inside of your door. May you bring that love and peace with you when you leave as well. Put all that you have to prayer, and unto the Most High, for HE is our YAH (GOD), and even unto HIS son, for Christ is our comforter.

Remain strong and be true.

S C R I P T U R E
MATTHEW 7:7
KING JAMES VERSION

7 Ask, and it shall be given you; seek, and ye shall find; knock, and it shall be opened unto you:

BE IN PEACE!

LIST OF SOURCES

- **The Holy Bible** (King James Version)
- **The Apocrypha** (King James Version)

Concerning new articles posted online and picture. I do not own any of the pictures used within this book, aside from the book covers.

CNN - John Agar - New York Times – Murderpedia - The GuardiaN – NOLA.com - Wikipedia

DEVRET CLARKE
BEHIND THESE DOORS
YOU REALLY DON'T KNOW ANYBODY

DEVRET CLARKE
TAKE UP THY CROSS

THE
NARROW
PATH
WRITTEN BY:
DEVRET CLARKE

We All Go Through It,
The Journey Called
"LIFE"
WRITTEN BY:
DEVRET CLARKE

THE RIGHTEOUS WALK
What Happened to Morals and Values ?
DEVRET CLARKE

DEVRET CLARKE
THROUGH THE STORM
THE BENEFITS OF
LONGSUFFERING

YOU
CAN'T
WIN
WITH
JEALOUSY
WRITTEN BY:
DEVRET CLARKE

WHAT
HAPPENED
TO THE
MANLY
MAN
?
DEVRET CLARKE

DEVRET CLARKE
No Sympathy
For The
Wicked

DEVRET CLARKE
EXPOSING
THE WAYS OF THE
WICKED

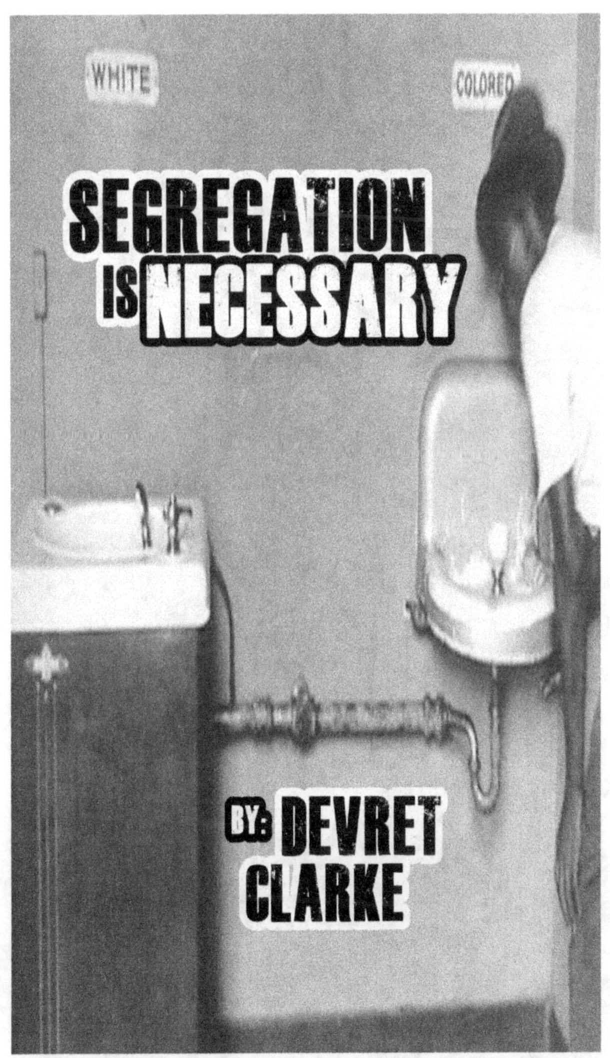
WHITE
COLORED
SEGREGATION IS NECESSARY
BY: DEVRET CLARKE

WHITE
COLORED
SEGREGATION IS NECESSARY 2
EXPOSING THE ENEMY
BY: DEVRET CLARKE

Still Sleeping?
WAKE UP!
Dedicated to the
12 TRIBES of
ISRAEL
WRITTEN BY:
DEVRET
CLARKE

Still Sleeping?
WAKE UP!
PART 2
WRITTEN BY:
DEVRET CLARKE
DEDICATED TO
THE 12 TRIBES OF
ISRAEL

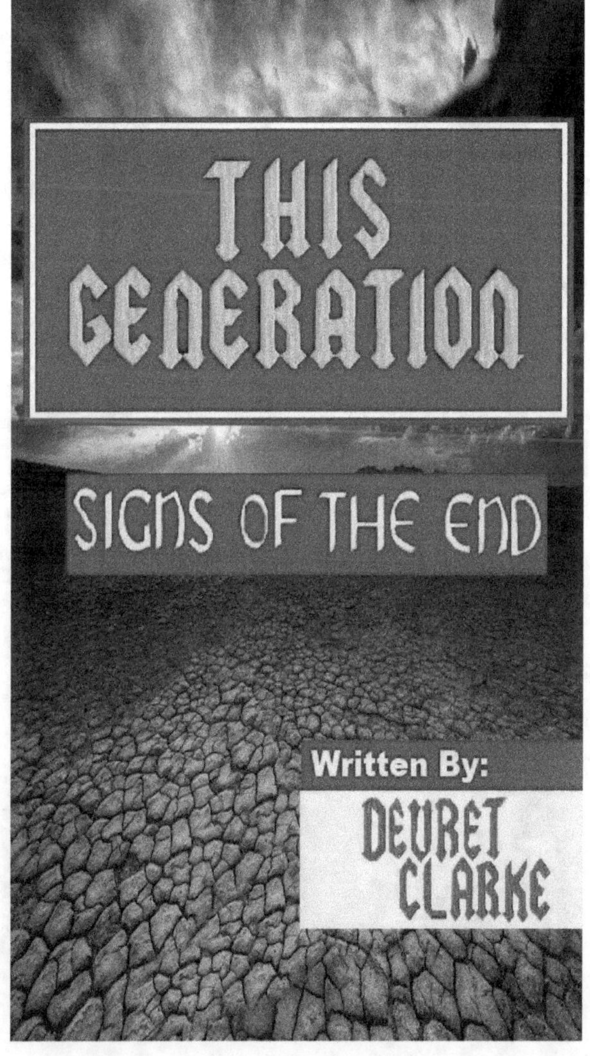
THIS
GENERATION

SIGNS OF THE END

Written By:

DEVRET
CLARKE

DEVRET
CLARKE
REAL TALK
JUST SPEAKING MY MIND

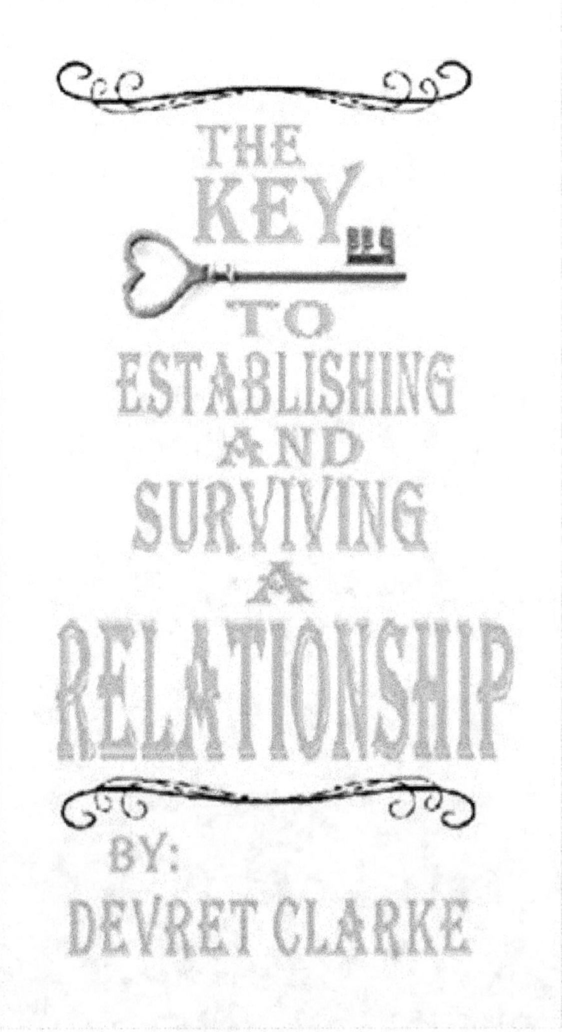
THE
KEY
TO
ESTABLISHING
AND
SURVIVING
A
RELATIONSHIP
BY:
DEVRET CLARKE

by: DEVRET CLARKE
LOVE IS NOT LOVE, UNTIL LOVE LOVES YOU...

DEVRET CLARKE
USED

DEVRET
CLARKE
BE
THE
EXAMPLE
NOT
THE
EXAMPLE

DeVReT CLaRKe
MIRRORS
Do you believe yourself?

DEVRET CLARKE
THE
INTERNET
ERROR
THE SURVIVAL OF HUMANITY

THE WAR OF WORDS
Written By:
Devret Clarke

THE
TEMPORARY
VOICES INSIDE
MY HEAD
Devret Clarke
Facing:
Unwanted Telepathy, witchcraft, sorcery, & "Gang-stalking"

KNOW WHEN TO RIDE
DEVRET CLARKE

Book Author's
DEVRET CLARKE
Website - DevretClarke.ca

Like what you read?
Support the author. All blessings are appreciated.

https://www.paypal.com/donate?
hosted_button_id=TMM43TPRV2VTN